Emerging Trends in Real Estate®

Contents

Editorial Leadership Team

Emerging Trends in Real Estate® 2011 Chairs
Patrick L. Phillips, Urban Land Institute
Mitchell M. Roschelle, PricewaterhouseCoopers

Author
Jonathan D. Miller

Principal Researchers and Advisers
Stephen Blank, Urban Land Institute
Charles J. DiRocco, Jr., PricewaterhouseCoopers
Dean Schwanke, Urban Land Institute

Senior Advisers
Christopher J. Potter, PricewaterhouseCoopers, Canada
Susan M. Smith, PricewaterhouseCoopers

Emeritus Emerging Trends Chairs
Patrick Leardo
Richard Rosan

PricewaterhouseCoopers Advisers and Researchers

Adam Harvey	James Pettigrew
Allen G. Baker	Jasen Kwong
Amedeo Prete	Jason Palmer
Ami J. Patel	Jeff Kiley
Amy E. Olson	Jeff Nasser
Andrew Alperstein	Jennifer A. Murray
Andrew Popert	Katherine Billings
Anne Daniel	Lois McCarron-McGuire
Brandon Bush	Lori-Ann Beausoleil
Bruce Raganold	Michael Chung
Chris Vangou	Michael Epstein
Christine Lattanzio	Nadja Ibrahim
Claude Gilbert	Nick Panagiotopoulos
Court Maton	Patricia Perruzza
Dan Crowley	Reginald Dean Barnett
Daniel D'Archivio	Rich Fournier
David E. Khan	Rob E. Sciaudone
David M. Voss	Russell Goodman
Dennis Johnson	Russell Sugar
Dominique Fortier	Sandra Blum
Douglas B. Struckman	Scott Williamson
Frank Magliocco	Stephen Shulman
Holly V. Allen	Susan Johnson
Ian Nelson	Timothy C. Conlon
Jaclyn Paul	Tori Lambert
Jag Patel	Yekaterina Kostyuk
James A. Oswald	

ULI Editorial and Production Staff
James Mulligan, Managing Editor/Manuscript Editor
Betsy Van Buskirk, Creative Director
Anne Morgan, Graphic Designer
Craig Chapman, Senior Director, Publishing Operations
Karrie Underwood, Administrative Coordinator

Executive Summary

After three years of dislocation and delaying unprecedented losses, the U.S. real estate industry finally sees some hopeful signs in 2011 of tempered improvement—across all markets and all property sectors. *Emerging Trends* interviewees expect halting advances in digging out from the recent avalanche of ill-considered commercial property investments and problem loans, but grow concerned about larger economic forces that could stunt any upturn and make the course more treacherous. "It's always been a mistake to bet against the U.S. economy," says an interviewee. "Just this time it's different. We haven't gone through a garden-variety recession, and now we're facing a huge deleveraging process, which means a subdued recovery." Worries mount that the nation and its real estate markets enter a disconcerting period of limits and uncertainty—an "Era of Less."

Among the anticipated factors slowing any rebound: unemployment stays high, wages stagnate, the middle class gets further pinched, lenders and regulators restrict credit, and the tax bite (including local property taxes) increases. The consequences of the nation's debt bomb explosion extend well beyond the obvious implications for this next real estate cycle, which include restrained revenue growth and tempered appreciation. The United States may have reached an inflection point where Americans' incomes and standard of living come under pressure in the face of intense global competition. While the population grows, individuals curb consumption out of necessity, and increase savings rates to ensure more secure financial futures.

As a result, developers realize "we won't need as much space" on a per-capita basis in the future, and continue on an enforced holiday. Technological advances and corporate outsourcing combine to moderate growth in demand for office space. Distribution advances and e-commerce reduce links in the supply chain between manufacturers and consumers, transforming warehouse needs and dampening tenant demand for bricks-and-mortar retail space. Homeowners slowly will accept that they can live comfortably and more affordably in smaller houses or apartments and gain economies from driving less. Infill areas and 24-hour neighborhoods in cities and urbanizing suburban nodes become more desirable locations for the large population cohorts of aging, empty-nest baby boomers and their young adult, echo boomer offspring. At the same time, fringe suburban subdivisions—long car rides from work, shopping, and recreation amenities—lose some appeal.

A flight to quality by investors accelerates toward the best places—typically coastal gateway cities with traditional 24-hour dynamics—further bolstering their investment citadel status. Many interior markets, meanwhile, struggle to attract investor interest; they typically lack direct links to global commerce pathways. More affordable communities face slower growth or worse because the incomes of people who live there may be increasingly compromised.

Lenders with strengthening balance sheets finally step up foreclosure activity and dispositions of properties during 2011 and 2012, helping values reset 30 to 50 percent below 2007 peaks. Borrowers should have improved chances to obtain refinancing, if they own relatively well-leased cash-flowing properties. But overleveraged owners dealing with high vacancies and rolling-down rents could face more uncertain prospects in the credit markets, including the increasing likelihood of foreclosure.

Investors with cash should have excellent opportunities to seize market-bottom plays by recapitalizing floundering owners and buying foreclosed assets, but they realize that pent-up equity demand for high-quality assets reduces chances for outsized returns. In certain 24-hour coastal markets, frenzied bidding for trophy office space and apartments already raises concern about buyers ignoring the realities of supply/demand fundamentals and conjuring unrealistic growth forecasts.

Survey respondents and interviewees ratchet down performance expectations, anticipating high-single-digit returns for core properties and midteen returns for higher-risk investments.

Without ample leverage (and attendant risk), real estate assets cannot sustain higher performance.

Washington, D.C., and New York City solidify ratings as the leading U.S. real estate investment markets, followed by San Francisco, Boston, and Seattle. All these metropolitan areas fit the *Emerging Trends* profile of 24-hour gateways along global pathways, which will continue to attract a large proportion of high-paying, brainpower jobs. Despite somewhat improved outlooks for all surveyed cities, most markets struggle with cash-strapped state and local governments and the prospect of reduced services, including police and fire protection and sanitation.

Apartments easily outrank all other property sectors: favorable demographics and the housing bust should increase renter demand, and some interviewees forecast rent spikes by 2012 in some infill markets where development activity has ground to a halt. Readily available financing from Fannie Mae and Freddie Mac bolsters buying activity. Core players also like warehouses and infill grocery-anchored retail, while full-service center-city hotels remain the top choice for opportunity investors. Suburban office gets the cold shoulder in surveys.

Canada's real estate markets largely avoided recessionary impacts, thanks to constrained lending practices and the dominance of conservative institutional owners who hold assets for cash flows. But interviewees remain concerned about lagging outlooks for the U.S. economy, which could impinge on Canada's growth track, especially for industrial and hotel investments. Most retail and office markets boast mid- to low-single-digit vacancies, and multifamily markets sustain strong demand. Toronto and Vancouver remain two of North America's most favored investment gateways.

Investors circumspectly consider Latin America's two prime emerging markets. Brazil, in particular, shows signs of becoming a major 21st-century global player, and Mexico's burgeoning middle class craves more housing and retail space.

Notice to Readers

Emerging Trends in Real Estate is a trends and forecast publication now in its 32nd edition, and is one of the most highly regarded and widely read forecast reports in the real estate industry. *Emerging Trends in Real Estate® 2011*, undertaken jointly by the Urban Land Institute and PricewaterhouseCoopers, provides an outlook on real estate investment and development trends, real estate finance and capital markets, property sectors, metropolitan areas, and other real estate issues throughout the United States, Canada, and Latin America.

Emerging Trends in Real Estate 2011 reflects the views of more than 875 individuals who completed surveys or were interviewed as a part of the research process for this report. The views expressed herein are obtained exclusively from these surveys and interviews, and do not express the opinions of either PwC or ULI. Interviewees and survey participants represent a wide range of industry experts, including investors, fund managers, developers, property companies, lenders, brokers, advisers and consultants. ULI and PwC researchers personally interviewed more than 275 individuals and survey responses were received from 600 individuals, whose company affiliations are broken down below.

Private Property Company or Developer	43.1%
Real Estate Service Firm	20.5%
Institutional/Equity Investor or Investment Manager	15.4%
Other (please specify)	10.0%
Bank, Lender, or Securitized Lender	4.9%
Homebuilder or Residential Land Developer	3.2%
Publicly Listed Property Company or REIT	2.9%

Throughout the publication, the views of interviewees and/or survey respondents have been presented as direct quotations from the participant without attribution to any particular participant. A list of the interview participants in this year's study appears at the end of this report. To all who helped, the Urban Land Institute and PricewaterhouseCoopers extend sincere thanks for sharing valuable time and expertise. Without the involvement of these many individuals, this report would not have been possible.

Entering the Era of Less

"The problems are obvious, but the solutions **oblique.**"

After a hard crash, the real estate world reluctantly enters a new "Era of Less" in 2011—encompassing a shrunken industry, lower return expectations, restrained development prospects, reduced credit availability, and crimped profits. Adding to unnerving short-term pessimism, commercial lenders and borrowers finally accelerate recognition of substantial losses (30 to 50 percent haircuts on asset values) from frenzied deal making in the years before the recent steep worldwide recession. Limping assets, suffering high vacancies and rolling-down rents, face problematic workouts and uncertain refinancing prospects as hundreds of billions of dollars of loans mature in each of the next four years, according to *Emerging Trends* interviewees. Housing, meanwhile, remains mired in a dead zone of reduced demand: many Americans cannot afford new homes even with record-low mortgage rates and slumping prices. But owners of the sliver of properties with healthy cash flows in prime gateway markets enjoy significantly better outlooks—a capital flight to quality buttresses prices and balance sheets—and, not surprisingly, everybody falls in love with rental apartments, the king of core-style income-generating investments.

Over the next year, some real estate players could gain significantly. The smart investors who sold near market tops, avoided overleveraging, and kept powder dry are extremely well positioned to take advantage of legions of credit-starved competitors who overborrowed and overpaid. Now, the haves can attract new capital, poach tenants, and lure talent away from the have-nots. Cash-flush investors and reviving lenders should have plenty of opportunities to recapitalize debt-starved, have-not players and take preferred investment or loan-to-own positions in asset capital stacks, eventually

reaping excellent risk-adjusted returns. For lenders back in the game and good-credit borrowers, the bottom of the cycle offers the best environment to employ leverage, especially on high-quality assets, and low interest rates only magnify the opportunity for owners. Investment managers and real estate investment trusts (REITs) with teams to lease properties and nurse asset income streams back to health can bulldoze aside many operator-light opportunity-fund boutiques, which had depended on cap-rate compression and leverage to reap appreciation. "You can no longer make money off flipping; you must be able to manage assets at the property level," an interviewee said.

EXHIBIT 1-1

NCREIF Capitalization Rates vs. S&P 500 Inverse P/E Ratio

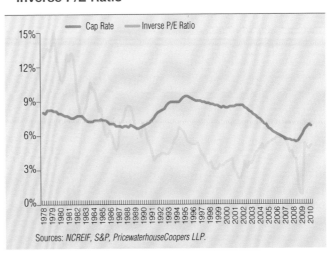

Sources: *NCREIF, S&P, PricewaterhouseCoopers LLP.*

Gradually, extreme negativity in the commercial real estate universe will abate. For 2011, debt markets will thaw further as money-center banks continue to strengthen balance sheets, take their losses, and step up lending, leading to higher transaction volumes. In addition, left-for-dead conduits will increase activity. *Emerging Trends* surveys also point to improved prospects off last year's rock bottom for all U.S. property markets and real estate sectors. This reconstituting marketplace should position real estate once again as an attractive yield-producing asset class for those investors who recalibrate investment expectations rationally. "The recent lesson learned is that real estate is a low-operating-leverage business," an interviewee explains. "It's very hard to get 15 percent to 20 percent rates of return without more risk and more leverage, and you can't succeed on a sustained basis. Real estate is more about cash flow and keeping buildings leased." What's wrong with delivering unlevered, high-single-digit returns or low-teens performance for conservatively financed assets? Well nothing, especially when you consider the dismal record of the stock market over the past decade.

Still, the overwhelming majority of *Emerging Trends* interviewees register doubts and uncertainty about the future and, especially, the subdued outlook for the U.S. economy, which not only flounders in consumer and government debt, but also struggles to create high-paying jobs in a more competitive, technology-enabled global marketplace. "Our problems are much bigger than real estate, and solutions are well beyond the scope of our industry." Americans and their government have been living large off borrowing for several decades, and now the staggering bills have come due. The housing debacle, precipitated by easy credit, shakes confidence to the core, undermining personal wealth and the sense of a secure financial future. Consumption takes a necessary breather as people retrench to pay off sizable debts—home mortgages, car loans, and credit cards—and increase savings rates from record-low levels.

The unemployment picture appears more worrisome: even before the recession, wages and benefits had stagnated for the average American. Manufacturing jobs have leached to lower-cost overseas markets since the 1970s, slowly decimating bedrock blue-color jobs. Now the internet and telecom advances allow companies to outsource more professional and service jobs to overseas locations at reduced wages, and various computer applications eliminate office and administrative positions. Many corporate productivity gains and enhanced profits come at the expense of damping down appetites for new hires, and now government belt tightening, especially at the state and local levels, eliminates more jobs as stimulus funding begins to run dry. At the same time,

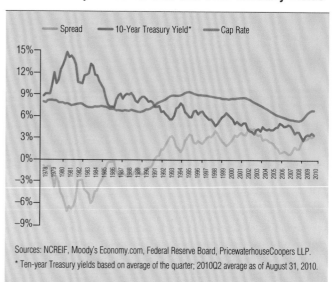

EXHIBIT 1-2

NCREIF Cap Rates vs. U.S. Ten-Year Treasury Yields

Sources: NCREIF, Moody's Economy.com, Federal Reserve Board, PricewaterhouseCoopers LLP.
* Ten-year Treasury yields based on average of the quarter; 2010Q2 average as of August 31, 2010.

corporations cut back on pensions, states grapple to reduce public employee benefits, and just about everyone pays more for health insurance coverage. Again this year, *Emerging Trends* interviewees enter a familiar echo chamber, repeating emphatically how real estate recovery "is all about jobs," but turn silent when trying to identify America's high-growth employment-creating industries of the future.

Homebuilding and commercial real estate construction certainly do not offer much hope for jump-starting employment or the economy in the near term. "We really don't need much new of anything." Housing led the economy into the dumpster, and increasing home loan defaults and foreclosures curtail any chance for a sudden rebound. Sobered lenders now expect homebuyers to make downpayments and have solid credit histories before they extend mortgages, but coming out of this recession, many Americans simply cannot meet these basic requirements or turn too skittish to take a chance.

Eventually population growth will absorb the overhang in housing supply, but location preferences show signs of shifting away from bigger homes on the suburban fringe to infill locations closer to 24-hour markets. Reversing decades of moving away from city centers, "more people will regroup in areas where life is easier, more efficient, and less car dependent"—that is, closer to shopping districts and workplaces. In the approaching cycle, the industry can expect to see more high-rise and mid-rise apartments, as well as townhouse projects, built around shopping centers and commercial districts. Failing retail space will be converted to other uses, often with

EXHIBIT 1-3
U.S. Real Estate Returns and Economic Growth

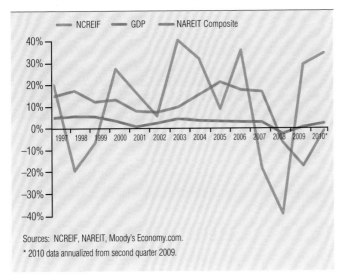

Sources: NCREIF, NAREIT, Moody's Economy.com.
* 2010 data annualized from second quarter 2009.

residential components, and more underoccupied suburban office campuses will be transformed into mixed-use properties. "Coming years will focus on readapting real estate to people's revised goals, priorities, and expectations. We'll be working longer, saving more, and looking for greater efficiencies in how we live and work."

Simply put, an Era of Less replaces an era of bigger and more.

Muddling Along at Bottom

A reluctance and sheer inability to confront the mountain of legacy asset problems, comprising hundreds of billions of dollars in investment losses, have hamstrung lenders, delayed market repricing, and hobbled chances for a faster real estate market upturn. The U.S. government talks a brave game about improved financial market stability, but keeps interest rates at "artificial" lows "to avoid more damage," and everyone worries that credit markets and world economies cannot endure the shock of wholesale asset writedowns. Despite widespread "extend and pretend" practices to avoid taking balance-sheet losses and force foreclosure on beleaguered borrowers, still-undercapitalized regional and local banks totter with overweightings of failed land and construction loans. Several hundred of these banks have collapsed into the hands of the Federal Deposit Insurance Corporation (FDIC), a process that will continue through 2011.

But buying time with extend and pretend may pay off for other financial institutions, including larger money-center banks and life insurers, as well as some commercial mortgage–backed securities (CMBS) special servicers. They will step up writedowns and workouts as a prelude to disposing of assets when loans mature, and likely can recoup some lost value in slowly improving markets. Given the looming number of maturing loans up for refinancing starting in 2011, this "painful" deleveraging to lower values and disposition process could take until mid-decade to complete. But with FDIC, bank, and special servicer sales, substantially more properties will hit transaction markets in 2011 and 2012, allowing the market to begin clearing and prices finally to reset. The time approaches to "absorb losses, deleverage to the new value levels, adjust, and move on."

No Way Out. In the meantime, compromised borrowers survive on life support until they succumb finally to maturity defaults or raise new capital from eager investors taking preferred positions. Essentially, "they get squashed." Most or all of their existing equity vaporizes ("If you can get back to par, it's a grand slam"), and some high-profile developers, who took recourse financing, suffer even greater carnage ("It's a personal wipeout"). Sentiment grows among *Emerging Trends* interviewees that odds improve for owners of properties with a reasonable cash flow to overcome refinancing hurdles as liquidity returns to debt markets. For investors in more commodity assets, whose cost basis goes back to 2005–2007 pricing peaks, refinancing prospects "hardly look rosy" as long as leases roll down to market rents and vacant space stays empty.

EXHIBIT 1-4
Emerging Trends Barometer 2011

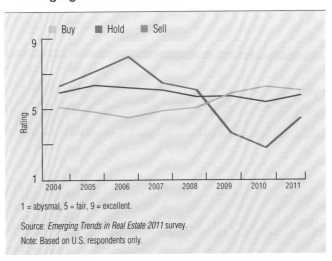

1 = abysmal, 5 = fair, 9 = excellent.

Source: *Emerging Trends in Real Estate 2011* survey.
Note: Based on U.S. respondents only.

Extreme Bifurcation. The capital flight to quality, predicted in last year's *Emerging Trends*, has produced "a deep canyon" separating "trophy" and "trash" assets, "with a lot more trash." "The best properties have cash flow, and that's what buyers and lenders want." Bifurcation results from investors protecting themselves against perceived risk in a problematic economy, and not as much from perceived opportunity and quick gains at cyclical depths. Investors have also learned from recent cycles that prime properties hold value better in downturns and appreciate more in good times. As a result, pent-up, sidelined capital swarms apartments and office buildings in gateway cities and mostly ignores just about everything else.

Increasing Transactions. Market bottom should be the best time to buy, finance, and set the stage for big investment gains. But buyers have been frustrated by lenders holding back on distressed sales, and bankers have no intention of forcing assets off their balance sheets until they have built up enough loss reserves. "Everyone waits for the dam to break." The *Emerging Trends* investment barometer indicates the gulf between buyers and sellers will start to close in 2011: selling sentiment improves dramatically from last year's all-time survey lows, and acquirers realize they should not expect giant discounts on everything that comes to market; in fact, buyer outlooks dip slightly (see exhibit 1-4). "Banks will start to sell, just not at ridiculously low prices buyers want," and as resources run out, "more borrowers will capitulate."

Already Overpaying? *Emerging Trends* interviewees' heads spin over the high prices plunked down for core properties in New York City and Washington, D.C., and "amazing" sub-5 cap rates achieved for some apartment deals. "Have people already forgotten what's happened over the past three years?" Capital appears disconnected from still-weak fundamentals, but historically rents can bounce back quickly in these markets, and demographic/housing–related trends strongly favor multifamily investments. Many buyers find justification in below-replacement-cost numbers, "but that's a useful rationale when economics don't support the purchase price." At these expensive levels, investors cannot afford any nasty surprises like double-dip recessions or out-of-the-blue events. Some private equity firms and investment managers appear to force out money before client commitment terms expire. "Instead of stretching on future assumptions" (didn't we learn this recent lesson at significant cost?), buyers should be underwriting on current income and think about exit caps when Treasury rates, now well below historic norms, are "sure to be higher." Investors also need to "resize cap-rate models to include more (30 to 40 percent) equity," replacing 90 percent debt. "Until people reconcile with the new reality, they could overpay."

Untouchables. At the other end of the spectrum, "the early stuff from banks has all sorts of problems"—properties "people don't want at almost any price." To move some of these "leasing-challenged properties" when buyers are experiencing the angst of economic doldrums, sellers will need to swallow hard and accept cents-on-the-dollar "RTC-style pricing."

Rational Returns. *Emerging Trends* surveys peg expected returns for calendar year 2011 in the high single digits—7.5 percent for institutional-quality private real estate equity (unlevered NCREIF) and 8.2 percent for REITs. These total returns comprise 5 to 7 percent from income and additional modest appreciation, and greater gains for signature properties in prime markets. "After a 30 percent to 40 percent loss, it could take a long time to make up ground." Opportunity investors may score on one-off deals, but will be hard pressed to realize consistent mid- to high-teens performance, especially in the absence of ample financing to fuel gains. If fund marketers create pro formas with returns above 20 percent, they either may be out of touch or trying to snow prospects, according to interviewees. Not surprisingly, survey respondents expect private equity real estate and public REITs to outperform the overall stock and bond markets—the professional real estate crowd always does. But publicly traded homebuilders will lag, according to surveys (see exhibit 1-6).

EXHIBIT 1-5
Index Returns: Real Estate vs. Stocks/Bonds

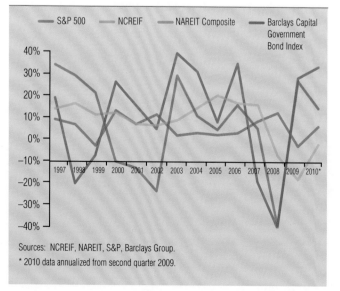

Sources: NCREIF, NAREIT, S&P, Barclays Group.
* 2010 data annualized from second quarter 2009.

EXHIBIT 1-6
Real Estate Business Prospects in 2011

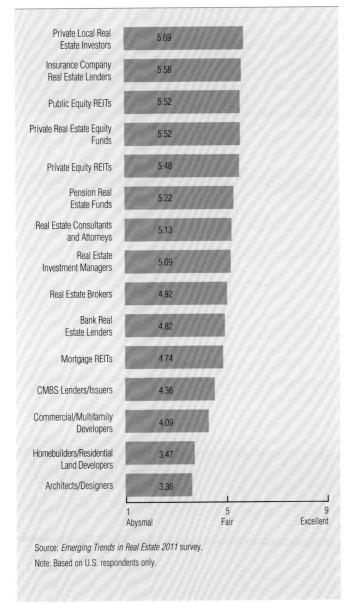

Private Local Real Estate Investors	5.69
Insurance Company Real Estate Lenders	5.58
Public Equity REITs	5.52
Private Real Estate Equity Funds	5.52
Private Equity REITs	5.48
Pension Real Estate Funds	5.22
Real Estate Consultants and Attorneys	5.13
Real Estate Investment Managers	5.09
Real Estate Brokers	4.92
Bank Real Estate Lenders	4.82
Mortgage REITs	4.74
CMBS Lenders/Issuers	4.36
Commercial/Multifamily Developers	4.09
Homebuilders/Residential Land Developers	3.47
Architects/Designers	3.36

```
1           5           9
Abysmal     Fair        Excellent
```

Source: *Emerging Trends in Real Estate 2011* survey.
Note: Based on U.S. respondents only.

Demand Drag: The Compromised Economy

For all the frustration about delays in market repricing and slow deal flow, *Emerging Trends* interviewees voice most concern about the shell-shocked U.S. economy and wonder if recent declines foreshadow a new age of diminished global clout and an ebbing standard of living. In these seemingly "unchartered waters," slackened demand for real estate across all sectors (except apartments) and near-record vacancies in many markets signal a long and difficult period before developers and landlords can enjoy any renewed pricing power, and one in which investors exercise little control. "The longer it takes for the economy to gain traction, the deeper the hole for real estate fundamentals to dig out." Outlooks range from mildly pessimistic ("the economy will rebound at some point") to grim ("it could be a ten-year valley"). Virtually nobody anticipates a sharp rebound: "They'd be brain-dead." Relative optimists hope for a U-shaped recovery, but a reversed J-shape seems more likely, and everybody prays to avoid a nasty double-dip recession. Huge deficits, ongoing wars, high unemployment, and consumer debt weigh down psyches. "We've bought everything we need for a while and now must pay off the enormous bills; the deleveraging will be extremely painful." And homeowners can no longer depend on rising house prices to cover spending. "People have been badly scarred by the decline in home values": for many families, the nest egg for economic security has been broken.

Flat Lining. Adding to festering consternation and dismay are business uncertainty over new government financial market regulations, the probability of higher taxes (including property levies) to fill yawning local-government budget gaps, and the breakdown of public pension systems. In increasing numbers, cash-stretched Americans must tap into their already meager 401(k) retirement accounts to meet monthly mortgage and credit-card bills. "When you visit other global regions, you realize the U.S. is not the center of the universe any longer or as dynamic," says an international funds manager. "We're headed along a lackluster plateau."

Hiring Malaise. More than any other issue, the sputtering U.S. jobs engine compromises sustained recovery and growth in real estate markets. People need the confidence provided by a steady paycheck to resume spending in shopping centers, look for new housing, and take vacations at resorts and hotels, while more hiring would help fill empty office space. But interviewees just "don't know where job growth is coming from" immediately, and they identify various hurdles:

■ "Many companies found they had a ton of overcapacity" and "the recession gave them cover to make cuts. Who says many of these jobs will be coming back?" Firms learn to operate with less and enhance profitability.

■ Lofty compensation and benefit rates make the United States less competitive against the rest of the world. The country has lost high-paying manufacturing jobs since the 1970s to Asia and Mexico, and many remaining factories have shifted from union bastions, mostly in the Midwest and Northeast, to lower-wage, right-to-work states in the South and Southwest.

■ Vaunted advances in technology improve productivity while taking away domestic jobs. U.S.-based companies can easily move operations overseas—call centers, financial analysis, software development, accounting, X-ray reading, etc. The internet and telecommunications make transferring information between continents seamless and instantaneous. CEOs and CFOs increasingly take advantage of "global jobs arbitrage" to increase profits and shareholder value, finding well-educated, English-speaking workforces to fill the demand offshore. "An infinite supply of service workers spreads beyond India to China and elsewhere and pressures down wage rates here." In short, what happened to manufacturing now happens in the service sector.

■ Technology has created new opportunities domestically in a range of brainpower, tech-related industries, but advances have also destroyed or drastically reduced the number of many traditional jobs that supported middle-class lifestyles—secretaries, file clerks, telephone operators, bookkeepers, order takers, travel agents, messengers, typesetters, newspaper reporters, and on and on. An executive with a Blackberry and a laptop needs a fraction of the office support he or she once did.

These same trends directly affect real estate owners, as do the following:

■ Midwest factory markets have been savaged by manufacturing declines, stagnating and shrinking through a chronic slump.

■ Internet shopping allows for more direct factory-to-consumer distribution without as many supply-chain links, leading to less need for warehouse space and fewer and/or smaller retail outlets.

■ Outsourcing of jobs overseas and/or to home-based freelancers dampens overall demand for office space, especially

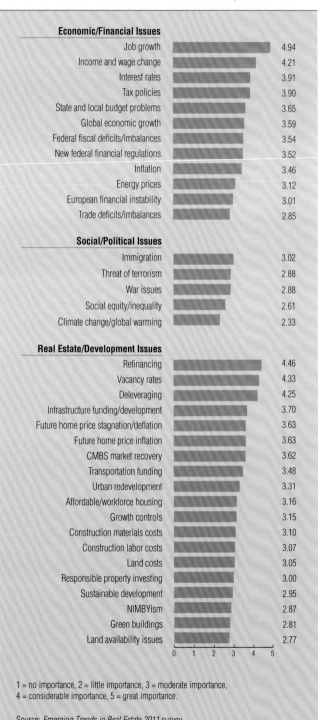

EXHIBIT 1-7

Importance of Various Trends/Issues/Problems for Real Estate Investment and Development 2011

Economic/Financial Issues

Job growth	4.94
Income and wage change	4.21
Interest rates	3.91
Tax policies	3.90
State and local budget problems	3.65
Global economic growth	3.59
Federal fiscal deficits/imbalances	3.54
New federal financial regulations	3.52
Inflation	3.46
Energy prices	3.12
European financial instability	3.01
Trade deficits/imbalances	2.85

Social/Political Issues

Immigration	3.02
Threat of terrorism	2.88
War issues	2.88
Social equity/inequality	2.61
Climate change/global warming	2.33

Real Estate/Development Issues

Refinancing	4.46
Vacancy rates	4.33
Deleveraging	4.25
Infrastructure funding/development	3.70
Future home price stagnation/deflation	3.63
Future home price inflation	3.63
CMBS market recovery	3.62
Transportation funding	3.48
Urban redevelopment	3.31
Affordable/workforce housing	3.16
Growth controls	3.15
Construction materials costs	3.10
Construction labor costs	3.07
Land costs	3.05
Responsible property investing	3.00
Sustainable development	2.95
NIMBYism	2.87
Green buildings	2.81
Land availability issues	2.77

1 = no importance, 2 = little importance, 3 = moderate importance, 4 = considerable importance, 5 = great importance.

Source: *Emerging Trends in Real Estate 2011* survey.

in secondary and tertiary markets, as well as in the suburbs of major cities.

"The bottom line is we need to create more jobs to drive the real estate economy and until we do, real estate economics will get worse"; just making up the 8.4 million jobs lost in the recession "will be a long haul." Logical growth sectors remain high tech and engineering, which need to create the new "new thing" to sell to the rest of the world; education, to help generate more higher-paid brainpower workers, especially in the tech, energy, and life science fields; health care, to address the bulge in aging demographic cohorts; and finance, to shelter and husband remaining wealth.

Necessary Austerity. Near-stagnant U.S. wages and the absence of free-flowing credit unsettle Americans while creating "strong headwinds" for maintaining the nation's upscale way of life. "Our gold standard may go down a notch." The United States will "remain at the top of the pile," but "lifestyles could ebb for the masses," creating winners and losers. Unhinged from charge cards and interest-only loans, people "must do more with what they have." As personal austerity becomes more of a reality, expectations adjust and frugality returns: "We're shifting away from defining success by how many toys we own." Twenty-four-hour markets attracting highly educated workforces and brainpower jobs will do better, but more commodity markets depending on lower-paying back-office, manufacturing, and service-sector employment could flag. "Six-figure salaries are alive and well in global pathway markets, but nothing's going on in many other cities." This "turn in the road happens gradually, playing out over coming decades": the credit crisis marked the beginning, and people are in reset mode, spending less and becoming more value oriented. Real estate players need to monitor how families cope. "Two-earner households allowed a middle-class existence; now we may need three." Grandparents, parents, and grandchildren may have to share resources and live together longer. Many graying baby boomers have insufficient retirement savings, and young adults, now struggling to find jobs, may have to downscale expectations.

Inflation versus Deflation and Higher Interest Rates

Record-low interest rates ("essentially zero") have been a lifeline to both real estate lenders and borrowers. Survey respondents expect rates to remain where they are through 2011 and expect inflation to stay under control for the year. But over the next five years, they forecast both higher rates and mounting inflation (see exhibit 1-8). "We're in such a big hole," the only way out is to print money. "The central bank will keep its foot on the gas to stimulate economic growth, putting people back to work and ultimately bringing on inflation."

Inflation Benefits. For the present, investors discount inflationary impacts and focus instead on getting yield, taking advantage of low financing rates if they can qualify to obtain credit. "Inflation may let you earn your way out of your loan, and a locked-in low rate could look good if interest rates increase later on." A gloomy minority of respondents contemplates a double-dip recession with accompanying depreciation, short-circuiting any nascent recovery. "If deflation

EXHIBIT 1-8

Inflation and Interest Rate Changes

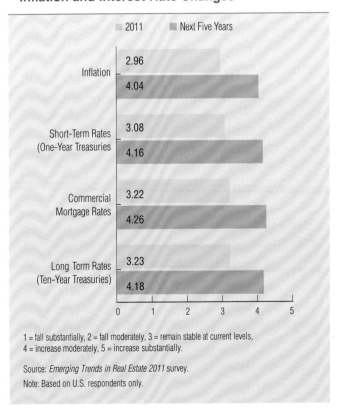

1 = fall substantially, 2 = fall moderately, 3 = remain stable at current levels,
4 = increase moderately, 5 = increase substantially.

Source: *Emerging Trends in Real Estate 2011* survey.

Note: Based on U.S. respondents only.

occurs, we're all in the wrong business," says an industry veteran. "But if inflation is coming, real estate is the right place to be, and it's time to get back in the game." Investment marketers may want to "dust off their old playbook" left over from the early 1980s touting the inflation-hedge benefits of property assets. "Over the next five years, that could help ignite transaction markets and put real estate back in vogue again." But an industry warhorse warns that inflation will not rescue property investments if demand does not escalate to absorb vacant space. "In the 1970s, double-digit inflation didn't help real estate, because of the oversupply."

Bubble Threat. A leading real estate economist raises a caution flag about an extended period of low interest rates. If yield-hungry investors continue to gravitate to the current attractive spreads between prime properties and Treasury bonds, an asset bubble could develop, leading to another sudden correction when rates inevitably increase. "It all depends on the Fed; we need to be careful."

Supply Side: Development Stall-Out

Absence of demand, rather than overdevelopment, has spurred record or near-record vacancies across many markets and asset sectors. "Fortunately, no new anything is coming on line, so when the economy improves, rents can start to increase more quickly." Overall, developers have little chance to obtain construction financing: most bankers assume the fetal position if a builder heads their way. But life insurers consider construction take-outs for apartment projects, if developers can provide enough equity—40 to 60 percent of cost. "Joint venture investments in apartment development can be better than buying," says an insurance executive. "Land is a quarter of peak value; construction costs are down 25 to 30 percent. You can make attractive investments in development on high-quality apartment or industrial properties, even with lower rents." A handful of singular office projects in site-constrained 24-hour markets can be expected to get funding, too, by year-end 2011, if the economy appears to be on sounder footing. These first-out-of-the-ground projects always score well early in sustained recoveries. Otherwise, the few office developments nationally will be limited to build-to-suit/net-lease deals and government buildings. "Rents just don't justify doing anything. It's dead."

Function over Form. For the future, office developers may look to cut costs by incorporating more modular, cookie-cutter, streamlined designs, offering different exterior finishes to tenants. "The future promises more value-oriented development," not ostentatious projects. "Tenants will emphasize function and efficiency, and green, energy-saving sustainability features will be expected."

Consolidation. Recessionary impacts continue to whack many undercapitalized developers. "Bigger companies have many more resources than smaller competitors." Survivors "need to deleverage further and protect equity for possible future shocks to the system." Some companies will merge and consolidate; weaker firms get folded into stronger platforms.

Regulation and Taxes

New Regulation Maze. Uncertainty over new financial industry regulation and future federal tax policy adds complexity and confusion to investment decision making, and many interviewees complain businesses "can't move aggressively on expansions and growth strategies," which might help fill buildings. "There are too many unknowns to make any decisions." Federal agencies scramble to write new banking rules—"the devil is in the details"—while lobbyists angle to gain favorable language (read: protect industry profits). Among the biggest outstanding issues will be how reserve requirements are meted out. Must CMBS loan originators retain a certain percentage of junior B tranches to ensure underwriting vigilance, or will CMBS 2.0 operate like CMBS 1.0 off moral hazard? Investment banks, meanwhile, position themselves to shed asset-management funds if reserve requirements seem too burdensome on co-invested house money.

Changing Tax Rates. Tax policy presents another investor conundrum, especially capital gains treatments. Investors want to keep long-term rates at current low levels, but the government desperately needs enhanced funding sources. Everyone grapples to secure new advantages or keep existing ones. "We need a tax policy to encourage long-term investing," says an exasperated developer/owner. "We should think about increasing shorter-term capital gains taxes and lowering long-term gains below current levels for extended holding periods. Right now there are no advantages to long-term investing, and assets like real estate are marginalized as a result. We trade and flip rather than build value over time."

EXHIBIT 1-9
Firm Profitability Forecast 2011

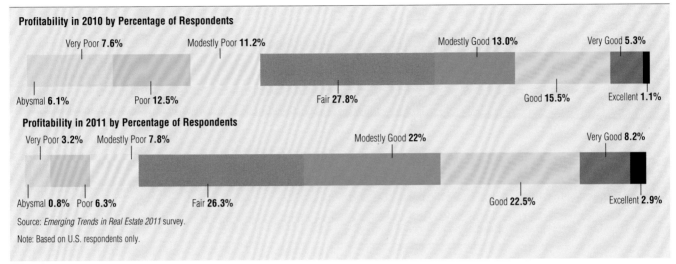

Profitability in 2010 by Percentage of Respondents

Very Poor **7.6%** Modestly Poor **11.2%** Modestly Good **13.0%** Very Good **5.3%**

Abysmal **6.1%** Poor **12.5%** Fair **27.8%** Good **15.5%** Excellent **1.1%**

Profitability in 2011 by Percentage of Respondents

Very Poor **3.2%** Modestly Poor **7.8%** Modestly Good **22%** Very Good **8.2%**

Abysmal **0.8%** Poor **6.3%** Fair **26.3%** Good **22.5%** Excellent **2.9%**

Source: *Emerging Trends in Real Estate 2011* survey.

Note: Based on U.S. respondents only.

Fannie/Freddie's Fate. At some point, Congress must come to grips with the future of Fannie Mae and Freddie Mac, the mortgage-market black holes, which prop up single-family and multifamily housing with hundreds of billions of dollars in federal infusions. Expected changes could make borrowing more expensive in the residential sector, and given the recent debacle, that may be a good outcome.

Real Estate Industry: Chastened and Smaller

While developers and homebuilders have been hammered uniformly, the rest of the real estate world struggles to revive in slimmer form. "A downsized industry feels more permanent than temporary," says an interviewee. "We don't need much new construction in any category"; commercial transaction activity was way out of kilter and will not ramp up to pre-downturn levels, and home mortgage financing volumes may take many years to recover to 2006 peaks. Deal makers, sales brokers, and mortgage brokers will not be in huge demand, although hiring is bound to pick up in 2011. Future deal making may not be as labor intensive or as profitable for brokerage firms. "It used to be you hired a broker for industry relationships to sell a property. Now you can reach the market effectively through a flyer to an e-mail list. Relationships are worth something, just not as much."

Survival of the Fittest. There is a shakeout among investment managers and private equity firms: poor performers flunk and lose business to stronger firms with broader asset-management and service platforms. Many opportunity investment managers leave the scene: they cannot wring promotes from legacy disasters, and their prospects for new investments remain limited without a bubble market and easy financing. Banks and special servicers still have trouble "building teams of experienced workout specialists"; if acquisitions pros want jobs, that is the place to go. Lawyers always seem to find ballast—shifting from closing transactions to handling litigation and negotiations between various stakeholders, trying to secure what is left from soured assets. On the leasing side, "brokers must have global coverage figured out to serve big companies." Owner reps will "work harder than ever before to find and keep tenants," while tenant brokers can exert plenty of leverage. "In this environment, career paths reward seasoned, experienced, plodding types rather than entrepreneurs."

Higher Profits. All the reconfiguring should help improve industry productivity and profitability from dismal nadirs, and, notably, survey respondents turn somewhat optimistic. More than 80 percent expect "fair" or better company profitability in 2011, up from 65 percent in 2010. And more than 30 percent predict a "good" to "excellent" year ahead. Less than 20 percent anticipate "modestly poor" or worse performance in 2011, compared with more than 35 percent in 2010 (see exhibit 1-9).

Best Bets 2011

Buying at or near cyclical bottom typically offers substantial opportunities, and 2011 is no different. But investors should be wary about obsolete and fringe assets, which have considerable downside risk even in recovery. "Sitting on hands" and waiting until the economy regains "certain vigor" still makes sense to more conservative *Emerging Trends* interviewees. And given longer-term trends, investors naturally should exercise greater circumspection. "You just can't throw dollars around in a time of slow growth."

Investment

Temper Expectations. "Don't try to shoot the lights out" and expect outsized returns. Buy well-leased core assets, looking for 6 to 7 percent cash flows. Appreciation will follow as markets improve. The best properties in the best markets always perform better whether over shorter or longer hold periods.

Lock In Leverage—If You Can. Mortgage rates cannot get much lower, and cyclical bottom is the optimal time to leverage properties in order to magnify future value gains as property fundamentals ameliorate.

Provide Debt and Recap Equity. Lenders only slowly reenter the market at a time when a flood of borrowers needs refinancing and recapitalizing. "Debt is scarce and dollars needed." Players who fill the gap on assets with lowered cost bases can obtain excellent risk-adjusted returns up and down the capital stack, including mezzanine debt and preferred equity, if not loan-to-own opportunities. "Concentrate on good assets with bad balance sheets."

Focus on Global Gateways, 24-hour Markets. Everybody wants to be in the primary coastal cities with international airport hubs. Business and commerce concentrate there, attracting more highly educated workers to higher-paying jobs. But high quality costs more, so prepare to pay up. When deals get too pricey, back off and move down the food chain.

Favor Infill over Fringe. Move-back-in trends gain force. Twenty-something echo boomers want to experience more vibrant urban areas where they can build careers, and their aging baby boomer parents look for greater convenience in downscaled lifestyles. Driving costs and lost time make outer suburbs less economical, while the big-house wave dissipates in the Era of Less.

Remember: Patience Is a Virtue. Transaction activity will increase, and more value-add and distressed deals will appear. "They're coming" as the pressure of time builds for lenders to push more failed properties into the market. Patient investors can be rewarded—"you'll get a better price per pound"—but buyers should have no illusions about rapidly improving revenues and a return to quick flipping. A slow-growth economy and more limited credit availability will not escalate pricing, except possibly in prime, flight-to-quality core markets. Familiar "hot-growth" Sunbelt cities may not enjoy a typical overheated expansion in any recovery.

Buy or Hold REITs. Do not expect another big run-up, but these companies appear well capitalized, can be accretive buyers, and concentrate strong core holdings in apartments and retail and office space. Liquidity is always a plus. Survey respondents expect solid cash-flowing returns.

Buy Land. It will not get any cheaper than it is now, but prepare to wait (a long time) for the right development opportunity. Infill sites hold greater promise than greenfield locations.

Exercise Caution on Distressed Loan Pools. "They could be a recipe for disaster," if you don't underwrite the assets properly. "Too many won't recover."

Development

Stay on Vacation. Except for some apartments, the odd warehouse, and select build-to-suit office projects, new construction activity will be basically nonexistent. "Why build when you can buy existing for so much less?" Demand for new premium product is probably "three to five years out," so plan accordingly and time recovery. Schedules for anything on the drawing board stretch out as the focus shifts to redevelopment and enhancement activity. Commercial developers should "think beyond the U.S.," looking to export talent to emerging markets that need new facilities. Homebuilders remain severely challenged: bulging inventories of existing houses hold back new construction, and prices continue to sink in some markets.

Property Sectors

Buy or Hold Multifamily. Rental apartments will outperform everything else. In addition to positive demographic trends, even the dampened recovery and housing market shambles are pluses because more people cannot afford to buy or stay in homes. "Subsidized" financing from Freddie and Fannie just ices the cake. Institutional buyers push up prices close to peaks in prime infill areas, and interviewees expect rent spikes by 2012.

Buy or Hold Select Retail. Infill shopping centers with top supermarket chains and fortress malls sustain performance through the consumer pullback. Darwin rules everywhere else in the oversupplied retail universe.

Buy or Hold 24-hour, Gateway Office. Premier downtown buildings remain investor mainstays in New York City, Washington, D.C., and the select few 24-hour markets situated along global pathways. Suburban office space outside urbanizing nodes gets a big thumbs-down in *Emerging Trends* surveys.

Buy Select Hotels. Always the most volatile property sector, hotels should be excellent buys at or near bottom. "They're the cheapest and will come back the fastest." Target downtown full-service hotels in major markets: many owners overleveraged late in the market cycle and are vulnerable. No one gets excited about high-capex resorts or limited-service brands in commodity areas.

Buy Condos and Single-Family Housing. Markets have collapsed, the population will increase, and demand will return eventually. Now is the time to buy your dream house, if you have enough cash. But this is not a speculator's market: do not expect a sudden future ramp-up in prices, except in the choicest urban neighborhoods and waterfront locations where values also tend to hold up better anyway. Avoid commodity, half-finished subdivisions in the suburban outer edge and McMansions; they are so yesterday. For good-credit borrowers, now is also the time to finance at locked-in, long-term rates.

Real Estate Capital Flows

"If you have a trophy property, lenders will come after you out of the woodwork. If you have a dog, you get foreclosed."

In the capital markets, the gulf between the haves and have-nots will become more apparent during 2011. The cash rich and well capitalized should feast off the cash poor and overleveraged. Big lenders should capture more market share, while more small banks nosedive into oblivion. If you are a borrower with bad credit, you're fried. If you are a buyer with dry powder, you should have plenty of options.

In 2011, the "huge spin game" of extend and pretend also finally starts to run its course. "We're deferring losses to build up capital, and we want to keep regulators off our backs by maintaining manageable capital ratios," says a leading lending executive. "Regulators know what is going on; [they] just don't want events to force them to notice. But at some point we will be able to take the losses and pull the trigger on writedowns, either when foreclosures can't be avoided or when it's time to refinance."

More Realistic

The odds increase that lenders will drop the hammer on troubled borrowers (the have-nots), and rationally leveraged owners (the haves) will be able to obtain precious refinancing when their loans reach maturity. It all depends on the quality of the asset and the prospects for improving cash flows. In a limbo zone between the haves and have-nots are the "have-lesses." "If you're not good enough to get refinanced and you're not bad enough to get foreclosed, you can get an extension, as long as you can cover debt service"—and live on to have your fate decided down the road. In any case, the debt capital markets become more liquid and get more realistic about asset values, setting the stage for champing-

at-the-bit equity players to launch into buying or recapitalizing more challenged properties.

Filling the Void. "Absent a major economic speed bump (like the dreaded double dip), there may be enough capital

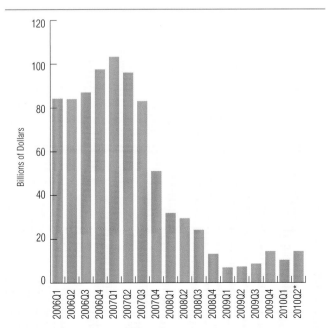

EXHIBIT 2-1
Sales of Large Commercial Properties

Source: Real Capital Analytics
Limited to properties $10 million or greater.   * Total through June 30, 2010.

EXHIBIT 2-2
CMBS Delinquency Rates

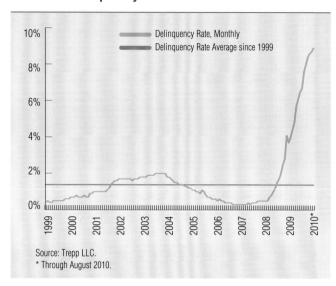

Delinquency Rate, Monthly
Delinquency Rate Average since 1999

Source: Trepp LLC.
* Through August 2010.

EXHIBIT 2-3
Real Estate Capital Market Balance Forecast for 2011

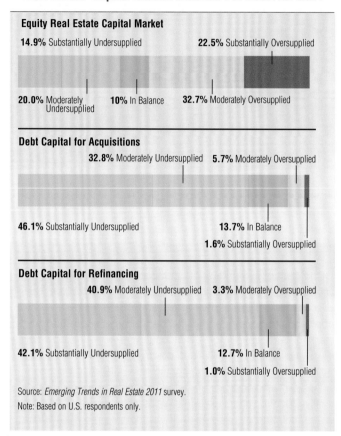

Equity Real Estate Capital Market

14.9% Substantially Undersupplied   **22.5%** Substantially Oversupplied

20.0% Moderately Undersupplied   **10%** In Balance   **32.7%** Moderately Oversupplied

Debt Capital for Acquisitions

32.8% Moderately Undersupplied   **5.7%** Moderately Oversupplied

46.1% Substantially Undersupplied   **13.7%** In Balance

1.6% Substantially Oversupplied

Debt Capital for Refinancing

40.9% Moderately Undersupplied   **3.3%** Moderately Oversupplied

42.1% Substantially Undersupplied   **12.7%** In Balance

1.0% Substantially Oversupplied

Source: *Emerging Trends in Real Estate 2011* survey.
Note: Based on U.S. respondents only.

for refinancing, as long as you have a decent property," confirms another lender. "Life insurers are fully engaged; banks will start to fill more of the void; new debt funds, sovereign wealth funds, and mortgage REITs will help; and, make no mistake, even conduits are coming back." But "realistically, it's a huge gap to fill."

Writedowns and Restructuring. Amid skyrocketing delinquencies (see exhibit 2-2), lenders and special servicers have already "started taking more writedowns" on discounted payoffs of debt, borrowers register losses so they can "raise cash to put out another fire," and new asset cost bases take into account higher vacancies and rolling-down rents. Workouts include earn-outs and hope notes; the key for lenders is "can the borrower pay something?" Loan-to-value (LTV) ratios are not as important. "Who really knows what the value of some of these assets is?" Where property metrics deteriorate in the face of tenant losses and borrowers run out of capital, lenders move more expeditiously to foreclose. "They realize it's better to take a hit and create a structure to stabilize the property than suffer greater losses." Banks will feed more distressed assets into sales markets as they can, but in the meantime, "financial structure right-sizing is happening."

Bigger Is Better. For new loans, "it's a very binary market where life companies kill each other to finance core properties" and most everything else goes wanting. The handful of "too-big-to-fail" money-center banks, buttressed by low interest rates and various federal infusions, will become more active. But back-in-the-game lenders will favor institutions and big-

ger players, and these already better-capitalized owners and buyers then take advantage of mortgage rates that are reasonable, thanks to Fed monetary policy. Smaller players more likely get left out in the cold. "The corporate guy can borrow a lot more," says a Texas sharpshooter. "REITs have a much bigger advantage in getting credit over the small guy."

Achilles' Heel. The brightening outlook for major market financial institutions and their better-capitalized clients does not necessarily extend to hobbled banks based in commodity markets. These regional and local banks, which serve less well-heeled investors, developers, and businesses, must "continue to kick the can down the road," surviving on low-interest-rate life support. Either their balance sheets improve or regulators take them over. "It's a failed business model," says a big banker. "Where do they get the money?" While these banks struggle to buy more time, it may be running out for some drowning in underwater construction and land loans to homebuilders and local developers, as well as a flood of defaulting home mortgages. If the housing market remains in

NEW EXHIBIT 2-4
Active Buyers/Acquirers of Real Estate in 2011

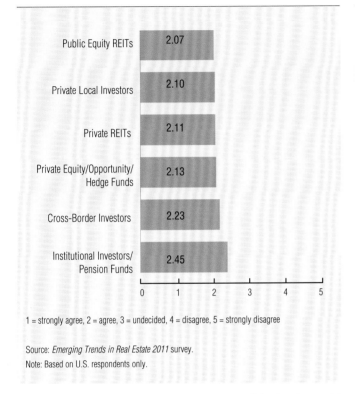

1 = strongly agree, 2 = agree, 3 = undecided, 4 = disagree, 5 = strongly disagree

Source: *Emerging Trends in Real Estate 2011* survey.
Note: Based on U.S. respondents only.

NEW EXHIBIT 2-5
Active Providers of Debt Capital in 2011

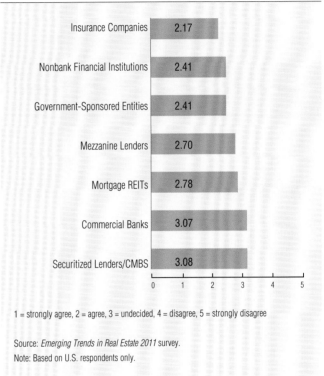

1 = strongly agree, 2 = agree, 3 = undecided, 4 = disagree, 5 = strongly disagree

Source: *Emerging Trends in Real Estate 2011* survey.
Note: Based on U.S. respondents only.

intensive care—a likely prospect—more small-fry banks could flatline, straining government agencies like the FDIC, limiting refinancing opportunities for their borrowers, and undermining chances for recovery.

Market Schizophrenia. *Emerging Trends* surveys capture the essence of market disconnect and bifurcation. More than 55 percent of respondents see equity capital moderately to substantially oversupplied for 2011—a reaction to the recent investment surge into a few 24-hour cities and the multifamily sector (see exhibit 2-3). They view this activity as a leading

indicator of the depth of sidelined equity "poised to pounce" back into the market, though they question the eagerness to pay up for properties so early in the cycle. But debt capital for both refinancing and acquisitions will continue in undersupply, according to surveys, a result that underscores an unsettling reality: there are many more troubled borrowers with "crappy assets" than rationally leveraged owners with solid properties. In 2011, REITs and well-capitalized private investors should have the best opportunities to take advantage of market imbalances (see exhibit 2-4). Life insurers are best positioned on the debt side.

EXHIBIT 2-6
Equity Underwriting Standards Forecast for the United States

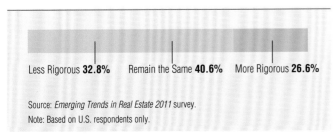

Less Rigorous **32.8%**   Remain the Same **40.6%**   More Rigorous **26.6%**

Source: *Emerging Trends in Real Estate 2011* survey.
Note: Based on U.S. respondents only.

EXHIBIT 2-7
Debt Underwriting Standards Forecast for the United States

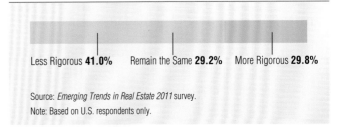

Less Rigorous **41.0%**   Remain the Same **29.2%**   More Rigorous **29.8%**

Source: *Emerging Trends in Real Estate 2011* survey.
Note: Based on U.S. respondents only.

Some Underwriting Slack. The degree of less-rigorous underwriting standards experienced in slowly thawing markets (see exhibits 2-6 and 2-7) depends on the condition of your financial institution and the state of your balance sheet. After "silence at the banker door" for more than two years, any attention extended to anxious borrowers signals some welcome loosening. Most lenders and equity investors "play it safe," steering clear of trouble, but they will continue to invest in top-tier assets and begin to underwrite more core-plus deals, as well as some value-add opportunities in the apartment sector. Aside from the frenzy over trophy institutional assets, lenders typically will demand significant equity downpayments (LTVs in the 50 to 65 percent range) and recourse.

Banks and Insurers

Without regulators breathing down their necks, the money-center banks will continue to develerage gradually, building loss reserves, stepping up writedowns, and lending more—mostly to high-credit-rating customers. They "assess asset by asset," preferring well-leased office properties and accommodating multifamily borrowers. But they shy away from hotels and show concern about retail. Some local and regional banks face more daunting challenges: outsized distressed debt portfolios deteriorate further without a vibrant employment outlook and improving demand for housing and commercial space. They cannot sustain restructuring or marking loans to market—"values have declined too much"—and they have little or no capital to refinance or make new loans. Investors waiting to gorge on bank

real estate–owned (REO) dispositions may continue to be disappointed until they reduce expectations. "If opportunity funds had a brain, they wouldn't be talking to us; they'd be talking to borrowers," says a money-center banker. "We're not sellers at their prices."

After a decade when banks and upstart conduits relegated insurers to minor status, conservative life companies "temporarily rule the roost" in commercial mortgage markets, and have homed in on their bread and butter—loans on trophy assets in larger markets. Insurers need "to get more dollars out" because the liabilities of favored annuity products match better to mortgages than did old-school whole life policies. An insurance executive admits to aggressive bidding on signature assets, "but getting a 4 percent or 5 percent rate spread with a mortgage looks relatively good compared to sitting on cash in money markets"; values were "so hammered on these properties, today's LTVs will look smart in a recovery." Insurers have also been able to attract borrowers willing to take higher rates than banks offer in return for nonrecourse loans.

Life companies have not escaped distress, but they have helped themselves by lending on a better class of property and dealing proactively with problems. Unlike banks, "we'll shift bad assets into equity portfolios more quickly and have been successful in pressuring borrowers into fronting capital to avoid foreclosures." Still, these institutions "bend over backwards" to avoid red-flagging nervous state regulators, who could raise capital reserve requirements. "Like banks, we don't want foreclosures on our books, and we'll make allowances to borrowers if we must." The life companies also

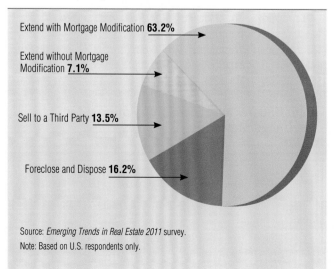

EXHIBIT 2-8
Maturing Loans: Preferred Strategy for Lenders by Mid-2011

Extend with Mortgage Modification **63.2%**

Extend without Mortgage Modification **7.1%**

Sell to a Third Party **13.5%**

Foreclose and Dispose **16.2%**

Source: *Emerging Trends in Real Estate 2011* survey.
Note: Based on U.S. respondents only.

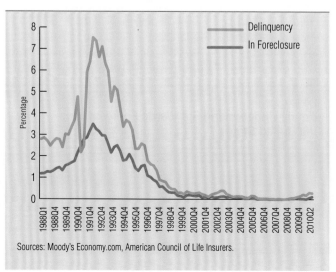

EXHIBIT 2-9
U.S. Life Insurance Company Mortgage Delinquency and In-Foreclosure Rates

Delinquency
In Foreclosure

Percentage

Sources: Moody's Economy.com, American Council of Life Insurers.

own large CMBS portfolios with plenty of bonds backed by thousands of assets "destined for distressed debt funds." "Nobody underwrote this stuff."

Wall Street

The big Wall Street investment banks look to regroup after taking the brunt of blame for directing capital into overheating property markets through complex securitized loan structures in what turned out to be a value mirage–inspired fee fest. Interviewees expect these firms to return in force once they figure out how to navigate federal regulatory reform. "Real estate needs capital, and the Street provides it." For starters, bankers structure new CMBS deals to kick-start the moribund mortgage securities market and watch for opportunities to take struggling private operators public. "They're resilient and will find a way to get their noses under the tent."

CMBS—Conduits and Special Servicers

Make no mistake: CMBS markets have begun to resuscitate. "They will come back slowly and gradually," says a leading workout specialist. "Teams are in place to begin originations and refinance, and there are plenty of dollars out there to

EXHIBIT 2-10
U.S. CMBS Issuance

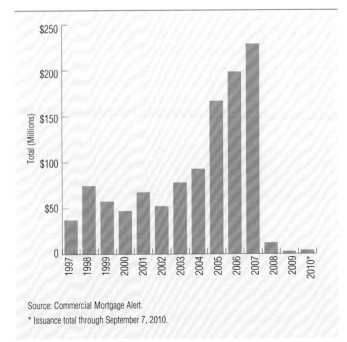

Source: Commercial Mortgage Alert.
* Issuance total through September 7, 2010.

start buying, but first you need properties to go through the washing machine and take losses. The game has started."

Various interviewees affirm outlooks for a revived $75 billion to $100 billion bond market "within a few years"—still far short of its $250 billion zenith in 2007. In the early going at least, loans will settle in the 70 to 75 percent LTV range, based on well-underwritten fundamentals. Major banks and investment banks will lead the way in putting together loan pools. New regulations will mandate greater disclosures to investors, who will "require originators to retain stakes in offerings." The big open regulatory question is whether federal agencies will mandate issuers and originators to retain stakes in B pieces, and how big those stakes will be. The industry argues that the market can dictate the process, but "obviously that didn't work" going into the crisis. "The only way to head off a repeat of the recent debacle is to require issuers to retain a percentage of each securitization and force underwriting discipline," argues an interviewee. "Rating agencies can't do the job": they were overwhelmed by the sheer volume of assets in offerings and have conflicts because sponsors pay their fees. Early next-generation CMBS offerings have focused on single-borrower portfolios, the same way "CMBS got kicked off in the mid-'90s."

Interviewees disagree over the impact of maturing CMBS loans on debt markets. Views range from "CMBS is the single biggest disruption" and "the black hole of refinancing," to the "wall of loans is overstated." But consensus reigns that "virtually any loan underwritten five years ago can't be refinanced at par." Borrowers complain that inundated special servicers will not address workout solutions for problem loans until a default, and "then it's too late" because tenants often have left and cash flows plummet further. While workouts happen, "special servicer hands are largely tied by what's in loan documents." They do not want to open themselves up to lawsuits. "Without a default and sale, it's very hard for them to take a discount on a securitized loan. What you'll see is increasing numbers of loans foreclosed and sold in an orderly fashion at distressed prices, but not huge numbers of restructures." Critics complain that special servicers ring up more asset-management fees the longer it takes to resolve problem loans. Recent acquisitions of special servicers by private equity firms with B-piece portfolios may "force action": these special servicers foreclose on more borrowers rather "than just sitting around, extending deals, and collecting fees." But interviewees point out conflicts. "They may hold off on foreclosing if their B pieces take too big a hit."

For years, *Emerging Trends* interviewees have predicted a mountain of lawsuits between tranche holders over failed CMBS investments. But so far only limited numbers of lawsuits have been filed, despite significant losses among bond

U.S. Real Estate Capital Sources

EXHIBIT 2-11

U.S. Real Estate Capital Flows 1998–2010

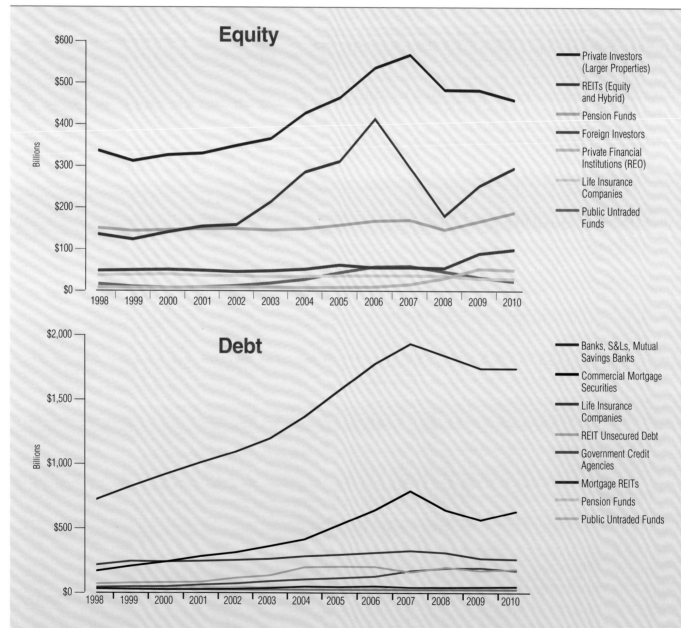

Sources: Roulac Global Places, from various sources, including American Council of Life Insurers, Commercial Mortgage Alert, Federal Reserve Board, FannieMae.com, IREI, NAREIT, PricewaterhouseCoopers, and Real Capital Analytics.

Note: Excludes corporate, nonprofit, and government equity real estate holdings, as well as single-family and owner-occupied residences.

*2010 figures are as of second quarter, or in some cases projected through second quarter.

EXHIBIT 2-18

Foreign Net Real Estate Investments in the United States by Property Type

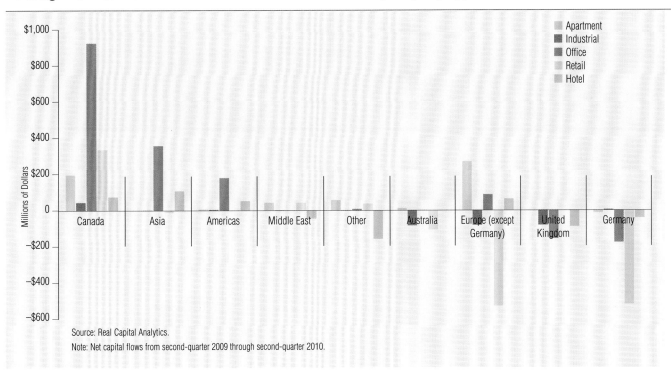

Source: Real Capital Analytics.
Note: Net capital flows from second-quarter 2009 through second-quarter 2010.

EXHIBIT 2-19

U.S. Buyers and Sellers: Net Capital Flows by Source and Property Sector

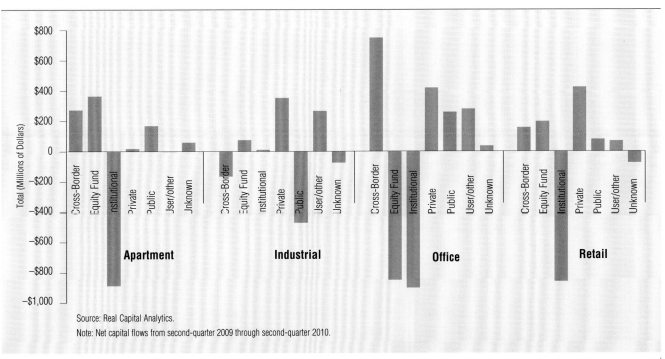

Source: Real Capital Analytics.
Note: Net capital flows from second-quarter 2009 through second-quarter 2010.

Markets to Watch

"Gateway 24-hour cities will always **dominate** and outshine secondary markets."

Economic doldrums bring the reality of the nation's real estate markets into sharper relief, "dominant institutional buyers concentrate on only eight or nine markets," and investors question the future of some secondary and tertiary metropolitan areas. If big corporate space users are any guide, "they're focusing on the places where they need to be," says a leading tenant rep. "They want the global gateway cities for headquarters and lower-cost Sunbelt cities with international airport access for back office." Strategically, they eliminate most everything else. Those cities left out will depend increasingly on government facilities, health care complexes, and education centers to secure economic prospects. "Accessibility and workforce are key. It's the yin and yang of links to global pathways—big airports, good labor pools, and company operations centers." Other interviewees suggest investors should "follow where educated, energetic, creative young people want to be." Inevitably, that path leads to the same group of highly favored metropolitan areas with 24-hour attributes.

No Surprises, Gaps Remain

Top *Emerging Trends* markets offer no surprises: Washington, D.C., and New York City pull away from the pack, followed by San Francisco, Boston, and Seattle. All qualify as preeminent gateway cities with attractive coastal (or near-coast) locations, barriers to entry, superior transportation hubs linked directly to global business centers, and concentrations of brainpower jobs. Houston and Denver also solidify rankings near the top, and respondents show faith in southern California's resilience, despite recent setbacks. While ratings improved over 2010's results for markets from coast to coast, the gap between top and bottom continues to widen, and more than 50 percent of surveyed cities still fall below "fair" ratings for commercial/multifamily investment prospects. "If you look market by market, you see some winners and more losers."

The Pittsburgh Scenario. "We're going to see a lot more places end up like Pittsburgh, if they're lucky," says a senior investment executive. "Here's a city that used to be a major manufacturing center with many corporate headquarters. Now it's cleaned up, the high-paying factory jobs have diminished dramatically, and a high ratio of workers have government or quasi-government jobs in education and medical fields." *Forbes* magazine ranked it as America's most livable city in 2010. However, "Property values and rents have essentially been flat and development has been sporadic." Pittsburgh ranks near the bottom on *Emerging Trends* surveys for investment and development prospects. Adds another interviewee, "Pittsburgh is a tight market, but stagnant. You can get decent, steady returns without much, if any, upside." And in the Era of Less, modest, boring income returns should become more expected, accepted, and necessarily embraced in more markets.

Better to No Prospects. Interviewees contend traditional interior, hot-growth cities can bounce back faster than many observers think, thanks to lower business costs and airports; Houston, Denver, and Dallas rate frequent mentions. Atlanta, another typically favored fast-growth center, draws less enthusiasm this year, despite its preeminent airport. Concerns grow

EXHIBIT 3-1
U.S. Markets to Watch: Commercial/Multifamily Investment

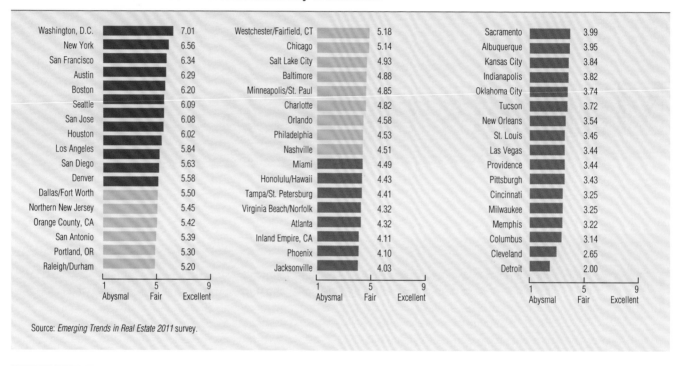

Washington, D.C.	7.01
New York	6.56
San Francisco	6.34
Austin	6.29
Boston	6.20
Seattle	6.09
San Jose	6.08
Houston	6.02
Los Angeles	5.84
San Diego	5.63
Denver	5.58
Dallas/Fort Worth	5.50
Northern New Jersey	5.45
Orange County, CA	5.42
San Antonio	5.39
Portland, OR	5.30
Raleigh/Durham	5.20

Westchester/Fairfield, CT	5.18
Chicago	5.14
Salt Lake City	4.93
Baltimore	4.88
Minneapolis/St. Paul	4.85
Charlotte	4.82
Orlando	4.58
Philadelphia	4.53
Nashville	4.51
Miami	4.49
Honolulu/Hawaii	4.43
Tampa/St. Petersburg	4.41
Virginia Beach/Norfolk	4.32
Atlanta	4.32
Inland Empire, CA	4.11
Phoenix	4.10
Jacksonville	4.03

Sacramento	3.99
Albuquerque	3.95
Kansas City	3.84
Indianapolis	3.82
Oklahoma City	3.74
Tucson	3.72
New Orleans	3.54
St. Louis	3.45
Las Vegas	3.44
Providence	3.44
Pittsburgh	3.43
Cincinnati	3.25
Milwaukee	3.25
Memphis	3.22
Columbus	3.14
Cleveland	2.65
Detroit	2.00

1 Abysmal 5 Fair 9 Excellent

Source: *Emerging Trends in Real Estate 2011* survey.

EXHIBIT 3-2
U.S. Markets to Watch: Commercial/Multifamily Development

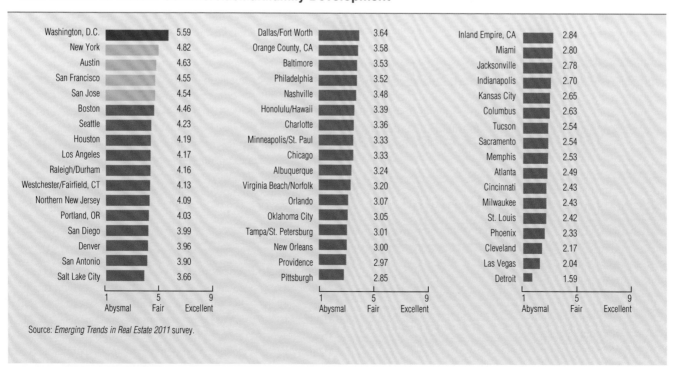

Washington, D.C.	5.59
New York	4.82
Austin	4.63
San Francisco	4.55
San Jose	4.54
Boston	4.46
Seattle	4.23
Houston	4.19
Los Angeles	4.17
Raleigh/Durham	4.16
Westchester/Fairfield, CT	4.13
Northern New Jersey	4.09
Portland, OR	4.03
San Diego	3.99
Denver	3.96
San Antonio	3.90
Salt Lake City	3.66

Dallas/Fort Worth	3.64
Orange County, CA	3.58
Baltimore	3.53
Philadelphia	3.52
Nashville	3.48
Honolulu/Hawaii	3.39
Charlotte	3.36
Minneapolis/St. Paul	3.33
Chicago	3.33
Albuquerque	3.24
Virginia Beach/Norfolk	3.20
Orlando	3.07
Oklahoma City	3.05
Tampa/St. Petersburg	3.01
New Orleans	3.00
Providence	2.97
Pittsburgh	2.85

Inland Empire, CA	2.84
Miami	2.80
Jacksonville	2.78
Indianapolis	2.70
Kansas City	2.65
Columbus	2.63
Tucson	2.54
Sacramento	2.54
Memphis	2.53
Atlanta	2.49
Cincinnati	2.43
Milwaukee	2.43
St. Louis	2.42
Phoenix	2.33
Cleveland	2.17
Las Vegas	2.04
Detroit	1.59

1 Abysmal 5 Fair 9 Excellent

Source: *Emerging Trends in Real Estate 2011* survey.

EXHIBIT 3-3

U.S. Markets to Watch: For-Sale Homebuilding

Market	Score		Market	Score		Market	Score
Washington, D.C.	5.86		Orange County, CA	4.08		Indianapolis	3.00
Austin	5.39		Charlotte	3.92		Inland Empire, CA	2.97
New York	5.33		Philadelphia	3.80		Pittsburgh	2.94
Houston	5.00		Salt Lake City	3.73		Miami	2.94
Boston	4.82		Minneapolis/St. Paul	3.72		New Orleans	2.92
San Francisco	4.78		Honolulu/Hawaii	3.71		Tucson	2.90
San Jose	4.57		Baltimore	3.66		Atlanta	2.87
Northern New Jersey	4.53		Orlando	3.55		Phoenix	2.87
San Antonio	4.52		Chicago	3.53		Columbus	2.76
Raleigh/Durham	4.49		Virginia Beach/Norfolk	3.50		Sacramento	2.69
Los Angeles	4.41		Nashville	3.49		St. Louis	2.65
Dallas/Fort Worth	4.35		Albuquerque	3.40		Memphis	2.62
Seattle	4.28		Oklahoma City	3.29		Milwaukee	2.58
Westchester/Fairfield, CT	4.28		Tampa/St. Petersburg	3.22		Cincinnati	2.47
San Diego	4.25		Jacksonville	3.22		Las Vegas	2.41
Portland, OR	4.16		Kansas City	3.11		Cleveland	2.36
Denver	4.13		Providence	3.06		Detroit	1.63

| 1 Abysmal | 5 Fair | 9 Excellent | | 1 Abysmal | 5 Fair | 9 Excellent | | 1 Abysmal | 5 Fair | 9 Excellent |

Source: *Emerging Trends in Real Estate 2011* survey.

about oversupply and inadequate road, transit, and water infrastructure. Overall, respondents remain negative about housing-bust markets in Florida and in the desert Southwest. And the Midwest's slow- to no-growth metro areas draw virtually no attention. Many secondary cities and most tertiary markets just do not appear on investor radar screens. "You see no demand, no capital, and no interest. There's no near term growth in office or retail and no need for new development." Local operators disagree, managing assets as long-term holds and focusing on owning the best properties in their markets. Inevitably, investor appetites will extend beyond the safest, major markets as economic recovery gains traction.

Budget Cuts. The nasty economy raises yellow flags for even dominant 24-hour markets. States and cities wallow in red ink; government lead-

ers have no choice but to raise taxes and cut services in already high-cost environments. Mass transit faces cutbacks while even police and fire protection and sanitation cannot escape the budget knife. "Every place has negative issues," "municipal risk over possible defaults is a growing concern," and "people will move away to lower-cost places." Twenty-four-hour cities rebounded in the 1990s when crime rates came down and streets got cleaner. Shrinking coffers signal trouble and possible regression if quality of life in these premium locations suffers significantly.

Rising Taxes, More Layoffs. Governments and taxpayers in places where property prices have declined significantly confront even greater challenges. Local officials squirm over raising property and sales taxes after real estate values dive. For the average taxpayer,

"that doesn't compute," and for commercial owners, larger tax bites crimp bottom lines even further. Interviewees point to "real estate taxes mushrooming well ahead of inflation," but "the problems are hard to fix." With federal stimulus funds running out, politicians look to avoid voter backlash. "We'll see more consolidations among local governments," more government-worker layoffs, outsourcing to private companies at lower wages, and pressure to reduce public pensions. It all adds up to more job losses and could put "more downward pressure on living standards."

Infill Gains over Suburbs. Some interviewees suggest higher taxes in cities and urbanizing suburbs could stall the trend of people returning to these higher-cost areas. But the overall residential tide is moving from fringe suburbs to urbanizing suburban nodes, and 24-hour downtown cores

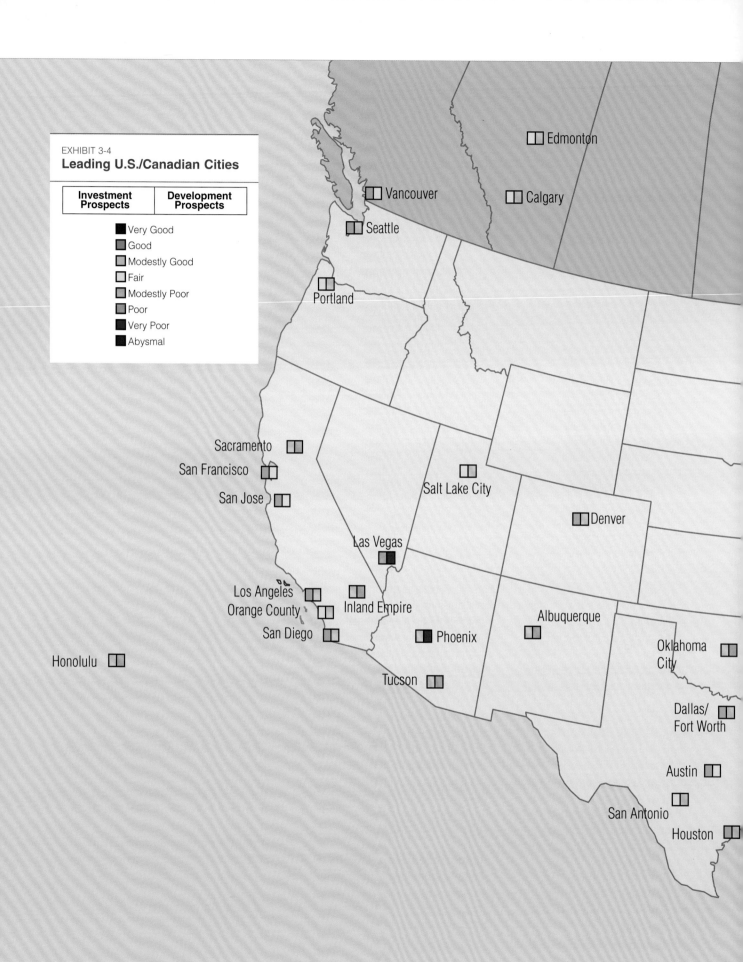

EXHIBIT 3-4
Leading U.S./Canadian Cities

Investment Prospects	Development Prospects
Very Good	
Good	
Modestly Good	
Fair	
Modestly Poor	
Poor	
Very Poor	
Abysmal	

Edmonton

Calgary

Vancouver

Seattle

Portland

Sacramento

San Francisco

San Jose

Salt Lake City

Denver

Las Vegas

Los Angeles

Orange County

Inland Empire

Albuquerque

San Diego

Phoenix

Oklahoma City

Honolulu

Tucson

Dallas/Fort Worth

Austin

San Antonio

Houston

Minneapolis/St. Paul

Milwaukee

Detroit

Chicago

Indianapolis

Columbus

Kansas City

St. Louis

Cincinnati

Nashville

Memphis

Atlanta

New Orleans

Jacksonville

Orlando

Tampa/St. Petersburg

Miami

Cleveland

Pittsburgh

Northern New Jersey

Toronto

Ottawa

Montreal

Halifax

Boston

Providence

Westchester/Fairfield

New York City

Philadelphia

Baltimore

Washington, D.C.

Virginia Beach/Norfolk

Raleigh/Durham

Charlotte

appear to gain momentum for other economic reasons. "You just can live more efficiently with less environmental impact in infill areas," says a developer. Bigger houses cost more to maintain, car expenses increase, and time lost in traffic and commuting mount. As a result, apartment and townhouse living near stores and attractions gains favor with aging, downsizing baby-boomer parents, and their children want "stimulating environments in more urban places." Subdivision-styled suburbs will not disappear, and schools will continue to be drivers in parent decisions of where to raise families. "But where are schools heading?" Will it matter as much where you are in the future? Will kids join classes from remote locations via computers and the internet and be taught by super teachers over the web? "It won't necessarily be the same." Some cities make strides in improving public schools and providing charter-school alternatives, while certain suburban districts falter under shrinking tax bases.

Infrastructure Neglect. Economic travail and government deficits distract attention from dealing with the nation's archaic and deteriorating infrastructure. Twentieth-century interstates and insufficient mass-transit systems can no longer support population growth and commerce in many increasingly clogged metropolitan areas. Newer Sunbelt cities, developed through road and highway grids, strangle in congestion while older 24-hour metro areas desperately need to replace crumbling bridges, overpasses, and tunnels. Water and sewage-treatment systems in many places age into inadequacy, while the nation's power grid dates to New Deal days. Financing a makeover will cost trillions of dollars over the next three decades—money the country does not have or does not want to spend. At some point, governments will be forced to institute various user fees and infrastructure taxes to pay for essential transport upgrades and new systems, including high-speed rail, light rail, subways, and airports. Eventual decisions and costs related to infrastructure could force monumental changes in where people choose to live and work.

Major Market Review

Washington, D.C. Never far from the top, the nation's capital will hold on to its number-one *Emerging Trends* ranking as long as the economy labors. The federal government never downsizes, while lobbyists and consultants swarm legislators and agencies hoping to influence or

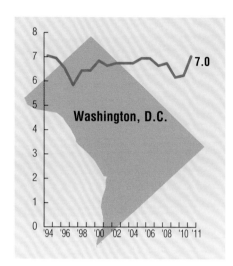

stop regulatory changes. All the activity cushions property markets and attracts investors. "It's a great long-term hold."

EXHIBIT 3-5

U.S. Apartment Buy/Hold/Sell Recommendations by Metro Area

	Buy	Hold	Sell
San Francisco	75.0	15.6	9.3
Los Angeles	73.2	18.7	8.0
New York	72.6	21.0	6.3
Washington, D.C.	69.0	21.0	10.0
Seattle	67.6	26.4	5.8
Denver	66.3	24.2	9.4
San Diego	65.6	21.8	12.5
Boston	63.2	28.7	8.0
Houston	52.7	29.7	17.5
Chicago	50.6	36.1	13.2
Dallas	47.0	29.4	23.5
Miami	38.2	39.5	22.2
Philadelphia	34.3	43.7	21.8
Phoenix	31.6	36.7	31.6
Atlanta	29.5	45.9	24.4

Source: *Emerging Trends in Real Estate 2011* survey.

Values "stayed within 10 percent of peak," so owners and lenders suffered "less pain," and no market benefits more from core buyers' recent flight to quality, driving prices back up. But interviewees warn the window for acquisitions has closed. "Pricing has been driven by false positives, too much money, and not enough fundamentals." In the survey, the District and environs also rank as the top development and homebuilding market, the top retail buy location, the third-best buy for office and hotels, and fourth best for apartments.

New York City. Who says bailouts and stimulus don't work? Troubled Assets Relief Program (TARP) and Fed funds directed at banks helped markets with financial services businesses and eased job cuts, benefiting New York City, which shows the biggest ratings jump in the survey over last year. Foreign investors remain active, "boosting market liquidity," and lenders loosen purse strings for owners of trophy office space. "You can get positive leverage on cheap debt." But sudden cap-rate compression "looks overdone," raising concerns of a forming pricing "bubblette." Tenants move to lock in rents before landlords get any pricing power: "They realize the market has turned." Office owners pull back on concessions

as rents trend up with more shadow space absorbed. Higher taxes to deal with budget shortfalls raise more shrugs than concerns from locals. "Everyone knows this is an expensive place to operate from, but they need to be here." Apartment rents rebound along with coop/condo prices, which registered only minor drops in the choicest neighborhoods, and retailers begin to fill in gaps in empty streetscape storefronts. New hotel completions could temper a recovery in occupancies and room rates, but tourists and business travelers are back in droves. Suburban markets generally lag well behind Manhattan; some catch-up will occur in 2011. The large northern New Jersey industrial market also strengthens with net absorption gains.

San Francisco. The country's most volatile 24-hour market, the City by the Bay now offers investors excellent near-market-bottom buying opportunities, particularly in apartments and hotels (*ET* survey number-one buy), office (*ET* number two), and retail (*ET* number three). The market also sidesteps some of its state's fiscal mess, performing better than southern California. Tech and life science industries flourish around top-flight universities (Stanford, University of California–Berkeley),

help attract brainpower, and sustain expensive regional living standards. Finance, international trade, and tourism further diversify an estimable business base. Office vacancies need to track down from the midteens, and veteran investors complain that current office rents stand about where they were in the 1980s. "You've got to be a market timer" to take advantage of boom/bust rent spikes. High for-sale housing costs make apartments an extremely desirable investment. Hotel occupancies improve and revenue per available room (RevPAR) should follow. San Jose struggles with oversupply, especially of new condos.

Boston. This venerable 24-hour city registers high marks for livability, controlled development, and a highly educated labor force, but lacks economic vibrancy. So join the club: that's the case for most markets after D.C. and New York City. Office rents did not precipitously drop off precrash 2007 highs, but remain well below 2000 peaks, and local brokers predict only a slight turnaround in 2011. Apartment rents will track back up—expensive for-sale housing keeps tenant demand high for multifamily units—and hotels show life. For the future, Boston should offer steady core returns with enough

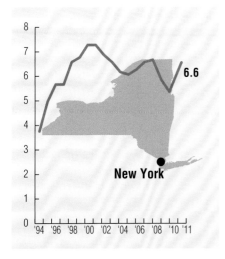

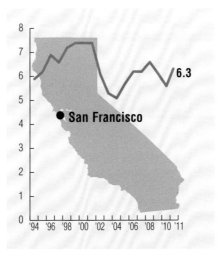

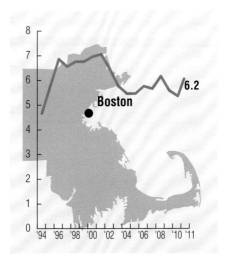

EXHIBIT 3-6

U.S. Industrial/Distribution Property Buy/Hold/Sell Recommendations by Metro Area

	Buy	Hold	Sell
Los Angeles	63.4	28.6	8.0
Dallas	56.6	33.7	9.6
Houston	52.1	40.9	7.0
Miami	52.1	36.6	11.3
Seattle	51.1	44.6	4.4
Washington, D.C.	48.8	37.2	14.0
San Francisco	48.6	41.9	9.5
Chicago	46.1	39.3	14.6
Denver	44.1	48.8	7.1
San Diego	38.8	47.5	13.8
New York	37.8	52.7	9.5
Boston	31.1	56.8	12.2
Phoenix	26.2	48.8	25.0
Atlanta	21.9	52.1	26.0
Philadelphia	20.4	53.1	26.5

Source: *Emerging Trends in Real Estate 2011* survey.

sustained buyer interest to bolster values and provide decent appreciation potential. It won't knock your "sox" off, but scores of colleges and universities, including Harvard and the Massachusetts Institute of Technology, establish the area as one of the world's preeminent knowledge centers. That is nothing to sell short.

Seattle. "Crawling out, but running on empty," Seattle gets a boost from in-migration to the area, "gaining 160,000 residents since the recession." Young workers attracted to tech firms want 24-hour lifestyles near where they work. "Big employers shift offices from suburban campuses to more infill locations,"

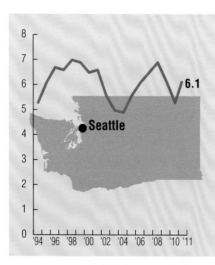

so perimeter areas find themselves increasingly left off the job growth path. Major employers like Amazon and Boeing "seem more upbeat," but "it's hard to see the economic drivers." "Microsoft is still right-sizing," and the state is broke: tax increases and service cuts, including public employee layoffs, lie ahead. "The ability to push rents will be more limited in the future." Despite vacancies in the upper teens after an ill-timed development spurt, office rents have held up, thanks to generous tenant improvement packages and what amounts to years in free rent. "Returns are abysmal." Overbuilt high-rise condominiums near downtown sit empty or half empty; developers take a bruising. Even with all the high-tech millionaires spawned locally, "just so many people around here can afford $1 million apartments." Industrial markets firm up at the bottom: the Puget Sound will continue to solidify its position as one of the nation's most important shipping hubs. Lackluster retail space does better, and apartment rents begin to increase with new arrivals filling units and construction languishing. "We've had the lowest delivery rates since the 1960s." Housing prices fell as much as 30 percent off record highs, but now prices tack back within more rational 15-year trend lines. "Place your bets on locations closer to the core."

Houston. "Out-of-towners don't get it": this city is hard to figure out. "We have no zoning, growth in all directions, and no barriers to entry." But market-timing developers always do well, and investors can achieve solid returns. "Jobs will always be here." Intellectual capital and talent in the global energy business concentrate in the city, the de-facto world oil and gas business capital, and Houston has one of the country's premier medical centers. NASA's downsizing plans and Continental Airlines' merger with United Airlines

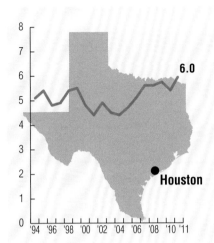

take the edge off office tenant demand. Nevertheless, downtown's vacancy rate in the low teens stands below the national average. The increasingly strategic port expands in preparation for augmented shipping traffic from the Pacific through the widened Panama Canal, scheduled for 2014. Population inflows help keep apartment occupancies up. Interviewees like the "business-friendly Texas government" and low taxes (no state income tax). "We should come out stronger from the recession than most other states, which creates more demand for real estate." Not unexpectedly, developers get ready to pick up any slack. "Build and sell quickly always makes for a good strategy in recovery." In Texas, builders can count on great demand, but over time, "rents don't do well" because of the constant new supply.

Los Angeles. *Emerging Trends* interviewees dump on California's high taxes and "antibusiness" environment—"the state government is a mess"—but also realize the "good opportunity to invest at insanely low values and ride out the storm." And who wants to bet southern California does not bounce back faster than many other markets? "It's an amazing place for multifamily": huge immigrant flows, high barriers

to entry, and large differentials in cost of living between housing and rentals keep apartment occupancies and rents high. Rebounding import/export activity lifts the outlook for distribution space serving the nation's largest port, encompassing Los Angeles–Long Beach. "Industrials definitely head in the right direction." Expected slow employment growth will not quickly absorb office vacancies, which average in the mid- to high teens areawide. Orange County looks especially soft: mainstay mortgage bankers and brokerage firms hit the skids in the housing bust. The closer to the coast, the better for investors: a housing free fall crushes areas around the Inland Empire and east of Interstate 5. Among the nation's over-

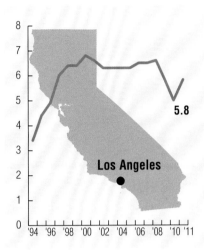

retailed markets, southern California's endless shopping strips may take the cake; a shakeout is underway. For all

EXHIBIT 3-7
U.S. Office Buy/Hold/Sell Recommendations by Metro Area

Metro Area	Buy	Hold	Sell
New York	64.9	26.8	8.3
San Francisco	62.5	29.4	8.1
Washington, D.C.	62.3	23.9	13.7
Boston	55.8	42.2	2.0
Los Angeles	45.2	41.3	13.5
Houston	44.8	37.9	17.2
Seattle	39.3	52.3	8.4
San Diego	35.6	51.1	13.3
Dallas	35.1	53.2	11.70
Denver	34.3	56.6	9.1
Chicago	23.6	54.9	21.6
Miami	21.1	55.3	23.7
Phoenix	20.6	39.1	40.2
Philadelphia	17.7	48.4	33.9
Atlanta	14.3	50.0	35.7

Source: *Emerging Trends in Real Estate 2011* survey.

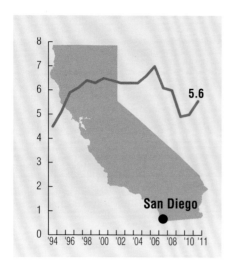

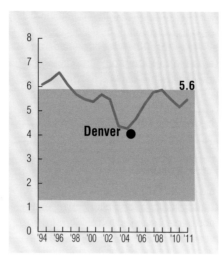

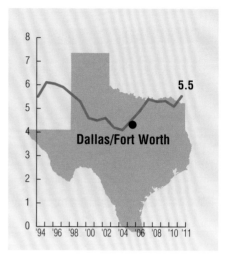

the negatives involving government gridlock and high cost of living, "people still want to live here." And don't forget that southern California remains the country's most important gateway to the Pacific Rim and Latin America.

San Diego. Ditto, ditto, ditto. San Diego's story largely copies that of Los Angeles. These two markets, not surprisingly, can track closely together. But San Diego does not rate L.A.'s gateway status, lacking a major port or international airport hub like LAX. "Traditionally, the local economy creates startup jobs, but doesn't retain headquarters. When companies get large, they leave." For global and domestic business, the city sits just outside primary jet ways, making travel a pain. As is the case everywhere else in southern California, housing prices have dropped from stratospheric levels, savaging mortgage holders. In particular, downtown condos are badly oversupplied. Demand builds back for housing in better neighborhoods: more buyers with cash want to take advantage of market bottom near Pacific coastlines. What's not to like about arguably the country's most desirable climate? Public-company homebuilders buy relatively cheap residential land to prepare for an eventual upturn. On the wobbly

retail front, put a hold on any more lifestyle centers.

Denver. The city makes progress positioning for 21st-century growth by strengthening its downtown core through a new light-rail and railroad hub to serve surrounding suburban nodes. As a result, the central business district becomes "the place to be," and mixed-use, transit-oriented development helps anchor suburban districts. This metro area also has one of the nation's most modern airports, an attractive Rocky Mountain backdrop, relatively low business taxes, and a broad-based economy anchored by oil and gas, alternative energy, and defense companies. "We can weather the storm better than most, and quality-of-life attributes will continue to attract people." In fact, the office market has stabilized, with overall vacancies in the mid- to high teens, and "larger blocks of space are (relatively) scarce." But it remains very much a tenant's market for users of smaller space: "10,000 square feet and below is a sweet spot for making deals." Apartment owners should see vacancies decline and rents tick up.

Dallas. Local developers learned from hard experience in the early 1990s not to take out recourse loans, and housing

prices never got out of control in the recent cycle. "The recession was not nearly as devastating here, and we're better off, but everything is soft." Dallas is always about strong demand and even bigger supply. "Every developer on the continent has an office there, so the market always has too much space." Companies like low costs, low taxes, and "a sizable labor pool" attracted to an area with an affordable cost of living. "You see many companies moving operations from the West Coast, getting away from a high-expense environment." Office vacancies have not dipped below 20 percent in more than a decade; perhaps with relatively tempered construction today, they have a shot to drop into the high teens over the next few years. Industrial space seems "okay, but never does well for long," once construction starts in earnest. Retail is more of the same: "been bad for a long time." Apartment builders can do well, constructing into growth waves, but investors in existing properties always face new competition. Dallas/Fort Worth International Airport remains this market's greatest asset, ensuring that Dallas remains an important intersection for global commerce.

Chicago. "We're struggling." Twenty-four-hour dynamics and O'Hare

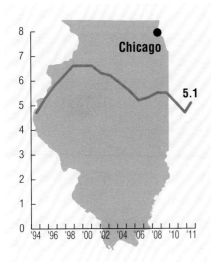

Philadelphia. Interviewees lament how this city "suffers from its proximity to New York," but others hope for gains from positioning as "a cheaper alternative." A bounty of superior colleges and universities anchors an attractive labor pool. "More kids going to school there stay after graduation." If only high-speed rail—traveling 150 miles per hour—could be developed to link with Manhattan, the city might get a major boost. Midteens office vacancy rates compare favorably with other cities, and locals tout the "good multifamily market." But institutional investors never muster much enthusiasm for the overall scene.

Miami. Interviewees resolutely express confidence that Florida can recover its

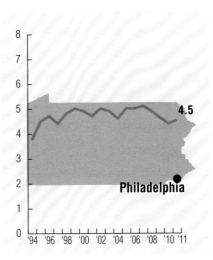

International Airport help maintain the city as an important interior U.S. gateway, but the ebbing fortunes of Midwest industries and slowing regionwide demographic trends diminish chances for a robust recovery. Only downtown Class A office space "holds its own"; the overall market rents have fluctuated anemically in the mid- to low $20s for years as developers keep building new upscale towers despite relatively weak growth. "Tomorrow has come to the suburbs," where vacancies, including shadow space, "approach 30 percent." Negative effective rents head lower as landlords try to stanch the bleeding. "Rates are likely to get worse before they get better." Most residential construction has stopped, but "the condo overhang" not only depresses coop/condo prices, but also holds down rents on apartments, "with no recovery in sight." Retail space and hotels are overbuilt, and industrial suffers from regional manufacturing flaccidness. Locals, meanwhile, find the condition of "state and municipal finances hugely troubling," weighing down the market with the likelihood of higher taxes and fewer services. And what happens after Mayor Richard Daley leaves office?

mojo. "The overall negativity hides some real bright spots." South Florida, in particular, lures global commerce and visitors, as well as baby-boomer retirees

EXHIBIT 3-8

U.S. Retail Buy/Hold/Sell Recommendations by Metro Area

	Buy	Hold	Sell
Washington, D.C.	50.5	40.2	9.3
New York	48.2	38.3	13.6
San Francisco	41.4	45.7	12.9
Los Angeles	36.1	49.1	14.8
Boston	31.7	56.1	12.2
Houston	29.7	56.8	13.5
San Diego	29.0	59.2	11.8
Chicago	27.8	61.1	11.1
Seattle	27.8	60.0	12.2
Denver	23.6	61.8	14.6
Miami	23.5	57.4	19.1
Dallas	23.2	59.8	17.1
Philadelphia	19.2	55.8	25.0
Phoenix	17.3	48.2	34.6
Atlanta	10.3	58.8	30.9

Source: *Emerging Trends in Real Estate 2011* survey.

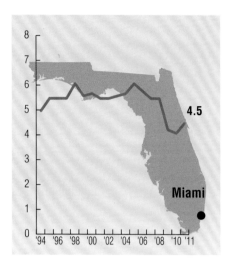

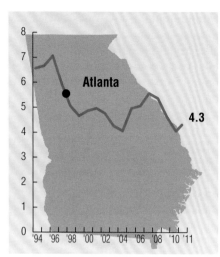

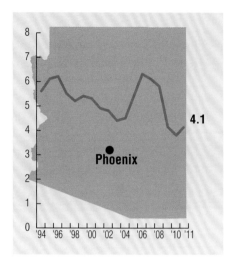

who gravitate to warmer climes. "This market has gone through cycles before and will attract a lot of people." In fact, South Americans and Europeans look for obvious bargains among the surfeit of near-empty, beachside condo towers. Buyer demand for rental apartments actually skyrockets, boosting values in expectation of meaningful rent increases. Some multifamily submarkets enjoy sub–5 percent vacancy, and landlords will be able to hike rates. Hotel occupancies and room rates have also climbed off the mat, but a moribund office market struggles with 20 percent–plus vacancy rates and declining rents, and housing remains a disaster area. Locked in by the ocean and the Everglades, built-out south Florida markets will have no choice but to build up and urbanize when expected population growth resumes.

Atlanta. Never your quintessential barriers-to-entry market, the metro area suffers from "overbuilding everywhere." Institutional investors "hold back for now; we've taken a hit and do not compare well against gateway markets." But boosters count many positives—a temperate Sunbelt climate; a world-

class airport adding a fifth runway; the lower-cost business environment of a right-to-work state; and a bevy of excellent universities, including Emory and Georgia Tech. The trend of people moving back to the cities is also alive and well, with more empty nesters and young adults relocating into urbanizing, infill districts—notably Midtown and Buckhead, as well as downtown neighborhoods. "We're finally achieving a critical mass of in-town living, and future growth will be concentrated toward the center." Unfortunately for many underwater developers and owners, these buyers and renters have too many cheap condos and apartments from which to choose. "There was too much in the pipeline when demand turned off" in every property sector. State and local governments "finally address" traffic issues, looking to expand highways with funding from increased sales taxes. The area also needs new reservoirs to sustain future growth. "We're trying to find a balance between funding infrastructure and keeping taxes down."

Phoenix. This growth-based desert city must rise from the ashes of another overbuilding spree, compounded

by deep recession. "It's a double whammy and will take time to recover." Everything is priced at "substantial discounts to replacement cost," and snowbirds can buy "ridiculously cheap" homes "where you can live like a king." Local investors count on people and businesses relocating from expensive coastal areas: "We're the first stop on the wagon train for people leaving California." But interviewees expect a "further downdraft in office," while the important lodging industry will be hurt by the ongoing "immigration imbroglio." Boycotts hit the convention business, and the area's low-cost immigrant labor pool runs for cover; "a major growth driver has been curtailed." New town centers "in every direction eat into mall shares." Like everywhere else, apartment rents should increase. For the longer term, the city wrestles with how to manage hoped-for growth and limited water resources.

EXHIBIT 3-9
U.S. Hotel Buy/Hold/Sell Recommendations by Metro Area

	Buy	Hold	Sell
San Francisco	57.0	34.9	8.1
New York	54.9	33.8	11.3
Washington, D.C.	52.1	34.3	13.7
San Diego	48.3	36.2	15.5
Los Angeles	44.0	42.7	13.3
Boston	41.9	43.6	14.5
Chicago	37.1	46.8	16.1
Seattle	35.3	54.4	10.3
Dallas	31.6	49.1	19.3
Miami	31.6	45.6	22.8
Denver	30.0	53.3	16.7
Houston	25.5	56.9	17.7
Philadelphia	18.4	44.9	36.7
Phoenix	18.0	44.3	37.7
Atlanta	14.3	42.9	42.9

Source: *Emerging Trends in Real Estate 2011* survey.

gridlock and potential state government downsizing. . . . **Albuquerque** will see relatively good job growth in 2011. . . . **Oklahoma City** benefits from reasonably high employment and the local energy business, as well as new downtown redevelopment initiatives. . . . **New Orleans** shows some signs of life as the post-Katrina infusion of dollars provides a modest payoff. . . . **Las Vegas** missed its bets, building too much just as the economy swooned. Competition from casinos, popping up nationwide, also erodes market share. . . . Ratings for many Midwest cities—**Kansas City, Indianapolis, St. Louis, Cincinnati, Milwaukee, Memphis, Columbus, Cleveland,** and **Detroit**—improve marginally, but national real estate players tend to stay away.

Other Market Prospects

Two smaller Texas markets receive relatively high ratings. "Everyone wants to live in **Austin**," the state capital, home to a major university (hook 'em, Horns), and one of the few cities in the Sunbelt with growth restrictions. **San Antonio** rates as "a good service market, but with limited rent growth potential." . . . **Portland, Oregon,** always gets high marks for quality of life, and its growth boundaries have encouraged a 24-hour dynamic in its downtown. . . . **Raleigh–Durham**'s research triangle concentrates brainpower jobs and, like **Charlotte**, will gain from continued population shifts to affordable, temperate regions. . . . **Salt Lake City** typically benefits when California hiccups. . . . **Minneapolis**'s diversified economy sustains its status as the second-best real estate market in the Midwest, while a new baseball stadium and expanded light-rail system strengthen the downtown core. . . . **Orlando**, **Tampa**, and **Jacksonville** creep off market bottoms; the Florida housing mess tempers outlooks. . . . Job growth in **Nashville** will bolster this market as tourism and other sectors recover. . . . If tourist traffic resumes, **Honolulu** will improve. . . . **Sacramento** bogs down in political

Property Types in Perspective

"After apartments, it's slim pickings."

For 2011, investment and development prospects improve across all property sectors after a hard landing in 2010 (see exhibit 4-1). Hotels actually show the greatest improvement over last year's dismal investment ratings, but only apartments register a good outlook. Highlighting the ongoing rush to income-producing core assets, survey respondents see modest recovery tracks for warehouses, downtown office properties, and neighborhood shopping centers, but more limited gains for malls, power centers, and especially suburban office property. Builders should take little solace from better—but generally poor—development ratings: only apartments warrant any possibility for new construction during the year, according to surveys.

Prospects Improve

Holding Tenants

In general, new leasing activity will occur "at substantially lower rates" than precrash levels, and rents will decline on average, except for multifamily. In the immediate future, "job number one is keeping properties leased and retaining tenants at almost any cost." Owners and managers must concentrate on cementing tenant relationships. Noted one interviewee: "The last thing you want to do is create a situation where the tenant isn't satisfied with the building. If the tenant is happy, then you can get down to economics." More tenants "renew and extend, which is good news, signaling confidence they can sustain their businesses and want to take advantage of lower rates." Expect some firming of rents in certain warehouse and downtown office markets during the year, but until then, many leasing efforts could end in land-

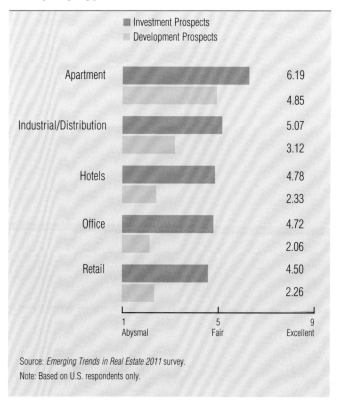

EXHIBIT 4-1

Prospects for Major Commercial/Multifamily Property Types in 2011

Investment Prospects
Development Prospects

Apartment	6.19
	4.85
Industrial/Distribution	5.07
	3.12
Hotels	4.78
	2.33
Office	4.72
	2.06
Retail	4.50
	2.26

1 Abysmal — 5 Fair — 9 Excellent

Source: *Emerging Trends in Real Estate 2011* survey.
Note: Based on U.S. respondents only.

EXHIBIT 4-2

Prospects for Commercial/Multifamily Subsectors in 2011

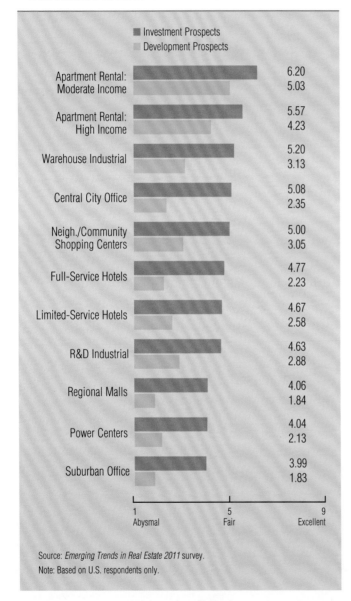

Investment Prospects
Development Prospects

Subsector	Investment	Development
Apartment Rental: Moderate Income	6.20	5.03
Apartment Rental: High Income	5.57	4.23
Warehouse Industrial	5.20	3.13
Central City Office	5.08	2.35
Neigh./Community Shopping Centers	5.00	3.05
Full-Service Hotels	4.77	2.23
Limited-Service Hotels	4.67	2.58
R&D Industrial	4.63	2.88
Regional Malls	4.06	1.84
Power Centers	4.04	2.13
Suburban Office	3.99	1.83

1 Abysmal   5 Fair   9 Excellent

Source: *Emerging Trends in Real Estate 2011* survey.
Note: Based on U.S. respondents only.

lord capitulation. Interviewees do not forecast upward pressure on commercial rents until 2012, and few expect spikes anytime soon. "Everybody adjusts to new rental rate realities."

Slower Demand Growth

Concerns increase over long-term demand trends. Tech advances and e-commerce affect not only retail, but also industrial and office sectors. More online shopping inevitably will reduce the number of bricks-and-mortar stores and enable more point-to-point shipping, modifying distribution models, reducing warehouse needs, and eliminating some middlemen, including certain retailers. Look what has already happened to booksellers, record stores, and movie rental outlets. Telecom and computer innovations make going to an office superfluous for more workers and enable domestic and offshore outsourcing to people operating from homes or at cheaper overseas locations. "It's a scary proposition long term since we may not see nearly as much demand growth."

Demographic Positives

On the other hand, the U.S. Census Bureau predicts the population of the United States will increase by 100 million over the next 30 years—or more than 3 million annually—necessarily boosting overall demand for various real estate uses, albeit probably at lower space-per-capita ratios. Ultimately these increases will help absorb excess housing inventory and propel greater demand for apartments. Arguably, a more frugal population will adapt to smaller, more efficient living units in areas more convenient to work, shopping, and recreation/entertainment districts.

What Is Core?

Perennially higher survey ratings for apartments and industrial space reinforce interviewee contentions that these property types are "the only reliable" cash-flowing real estate asset categories suitable for core investors. "Other sectors have more volatility than people want to admit." Class A office buildings in top gateway markets, dominant fortress malls, and prime neighborhood shopping centers in solid infill neighborhoods might also qualify as dependable core real estate. However, other property subsectors miss the cut, including commodity suburban office buildings, the average shopping center strip, the typical power center, and lower-quality regional shopping malls. Hotels never make the list: they have always been rated too volatile to fit into core portfolios.

EXHIBIT 4-3

Prospects for Capitalization Rates

Property Type	Cap Rate August 2010 (Percent)	Expected Cap Rate December 2011 (Percent)	Expected Cap Rate Shift (Basis Points)
Apartment Rental: Moderate Income	6.71	6.36	-35
Apartment Rental: High Income	6.39	6.65	+26
Central City Office	7.10	7.09	-1
Regional Malls	7.21	7.20	-1
R&D Industrial	8.26	7.59	-67
Neigh./Community Shopping Centers	7.70	7.61	-8
Warehouse Industrial	7.75	7.75	0
Power Centers	8.11	8.12	+2
Suburban Office	8.40	8.32	-8
Full-Service Hotels	8.73	8.67	-6
Limited-Service Hotels	9.21	9.00	-21

Source: *Emerging Trends in Real Estate 2011* survey.

Note: Based on U.S. respondents only.

Cap Rates

Expected cap rate moves through year-end 2011 indicate an overall stable to downward shift as demand strengthens across most property sectors in a slow recovery (see exhibit 4-3). Not surprisingly, apartments score the lowest rates, followed by central city office, research and development industrial, neighborhood retail, and warehouse industrial. At the high end are limited-service and full-service hotels, followed by suburban office.

More Green

While office developers and owners hunker down, they come to accept that sustainable building concepts will become standard in next-generation projects and that many existing buildings will need to increase efficiencies and retrofit new systems in order to compete effectively. "Green is here to stay since large corporations and government operations now demand it" and more cities build requirements into local codes. "Every owner needs to be on top of the issue." "If it's a green versus brown building, green has the edge." For now, many overstretched landlords with compromised asset structures cannot afford to address green issues, and most tenants, looking for rent concessions, will not pay more for sustainable systems even though they want them. "Over the next five to ten years, green will turn into a major trend," says a developer. "The math and savings achieved will start to make sense and bring landlords and tenants together, with government regulations forcing the issue."

Fits and Starts

Relatively short-term holding periods and profit imperatives deter some investors and corporate owners from making green enhancements. "Waiting ten years for a full payback to green investment can be a turnoff." But the cost of retrofitting buildings could be repaid from energy savings, possibly aided by some form of government tax credit tied to creating new jobs. Many owners find they can "game" the Leadership in Energy and Environmental Design (LEED) rating system "without spending too much" through cosmetic changes like adding bike racks and simply changing to more energy-efficient lightbulbs. But tenants become more sophisticated in identifying the "window dressing." Although it is hard to quantify green benefits, when tenants see them, they recognize them and want the associated productivity, efficiency, and image enhancement. "It's like buying a 25-year-old car versus a new model." On the residential side, investors and owners express more interest in reducing and managing energy costs than renters do. And so far, "formaldehyde-free cabinets" have not caught on in any marketing campaigns for new condos.

Mixed Use

During the building hiatus, developers also consider the future of mixed-use projects. Many stand-alone developments in car-dependent suburban areas have had problematic outcomes. For mixed-use development to work, projects must be part of larger town centers or urbanizing districts. "Just building residential over retail can be difficult, but works better in infill locations." In more suburban office districts, office/hotel/retail developments gain a significant advantage over stand-alone office parks. "Younger professionals want walkable centers where they don't have to get into a car to have lunch or do errands," says a Sunbelt developer. "Typical office parks have a commodity flavor where it's hard to distinguish between them." Probably the most significant mixed-use trend involves building more mid- and high-rise residential around established regional shopping centers, as well as incorporating office space and hotels. What were billed in the 1970s and 1980s as America's new town centers finally transform into pedestrian-friendly urban cores.

EXHIBIT 4-4

U.S. Apartment Investment Prospect Trends

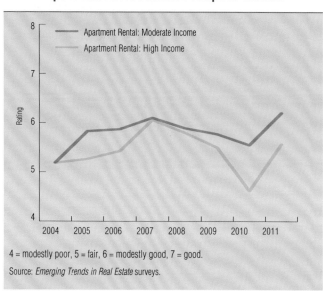

Apartment Rental: Moderate Income
Apartment Rental: High Income

4 = modestly poor, 5 = fair, 6 = modestly good, 7 = good.

Source: *Emerging Trends in Real Estate* surveys.

EXHIBIT 4-5

U.S. Moderate-Income Apartments

2011	Prospects	Rating	Ranking
Investment Prospects	Modestly Good	6.20	1st
Development Prospects	Fair	5.03	1st
Expected Capitalization Rate, December 2010		6.4%	

Buy	Hold	Sell
59.8%	28.6%	11.6%

Source: *Emerging Trends in Real Estate 2011* survey.
Note: Based on U.S. responses only.

EXHIBIT 4-6

U.S. High-Income Apartments

2011	Prospects	Rating	Ranking
Investment Prospects	Modestly Good	5.57	2nd
Development Prospects	Modestly Poor	4.23	2nd
Expected Capitalization Rate, December 2010		6.6%	

Buy	Hold	Sell
28.9%	52.4%	18.8%

Source: *Emerging Trends in Real Estate 2011* survey.
Note: Based on U.S. responses only.

Apartments

Strengths

Everybody loves "low beta" apartments—"the safest bet" through the cycle. Once the province of "sleazy syndicators," multifamily investments morph into "the new gold standard" for institutional property portfolios. All the stars begin to align. Severely constrained recent development plus pent-up demand from the burgeoning young-adult population cohort and busted homeowners back in the rental market add up to lowered vacancies and eventual rent hikes. "You sense improving fundamentals with legs at least to mid-decade." In addition, Fannie Mae and Freddie Mac effectively subsidize financing. Ready leverage at or near market bottom could turbocharge returns in the up cycle. "There's no way you'd pay [current] prices without low rates and available financing." For the longer term, apartments appear well positioned to adjust rents quickly if inflation kicks in.

Weaknesses

Swelling demand in the flight to core real estate compresses apartment cap rates to uncomfortably low levels—down 200 basis points in some markets. "Anything top quality gets people frenzied." Interviewees worry prices have increased too much too soon, and cap rates could back up, especially for high-income apartments in markets where more condos

EXHIBIT 4-7

U.S. Multifamily Completions and Vacancy Rates

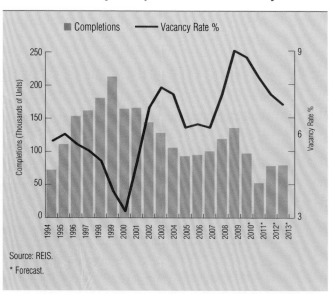

Completions   Vacancy Rate %

Source: REIS.
* Forecast.

will convert into rentals—Las Vegas, Florida coastline cities, and Atlanta. Investors also need caution in suburban markets where for-sale housing turns into rentals and competes for tenants. In addition, multifamily players worry about the future of Fannie and Freddie, depending on what Congress decides to do with the failed lenders. "Any reformulation will raise spreads, and originators must have more skin in the game."

Best Bets

Sellers with established assets can reap big gains. But why sell if you have a good income generator that should improve when the economy gets untracked? Barrier-to-entry markets, particularly the 24-hour metro areas, offer excellent opportunities, but expect plenty of company in any bidding. Value-add investors can boost performance through classic fix-up strategies on older product as markets improve and tenant demand intensifies.

Avoid

Sidestep older apartments in commodity suburban districts where developers can easily build new product. It is harder to raise rents, and maintenance costs can eat into restrained revenues.

EXHIBIT 4-8
U.S. Apartment Property Total Returns

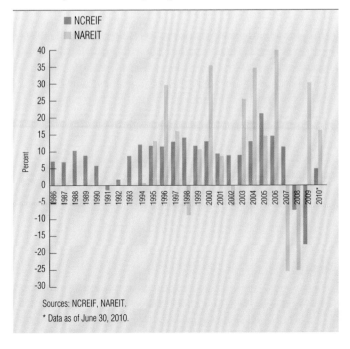

Sources: NCREIF, NAREIT.
* Data as of June 30, 2010.

Development

Low cap rates on existing apartments "open the door to new construction." In some markets, "you can develop for less than buying." Construction financing could be an obstacle, but life insurers and banks will step up if developers provide enough equity and go recourse. Expect apartment REITs to start projects, taking advantage of credit lines and superior balance-sheet positions to obtain financing.

Outlook

People need a place to sleep and look for greater economies. In the Era of Less, apartments fit the bill. Since couples marry and start families later, homebuying inclinations from generation Y/echo boomers will not stir and intensify for another ten years. Until then, this large population cohort will rent as they build careers. More downsizing seniors will choose apartment lifestyles, too, living off proceeds from house sales. As long as developers and construction lenders check their appetites, apartment investors should benefit "with the wind at their backs."

Industrial

Strengths

Despite record-high vacancies and continuing rent drops, warehouse properties sustain solid support from investors, who believe in their long-term revenue-generating characteristics. More than 90 percent of *Emerging Trends* survey respondents favor buying or holding warehouses in 2011, and the sector almost always garners higher ratings than any other category except apartments. This capital support helps shore up values and mitigates losses in downturns. Shipping and trade activity show signs of modest improvement as business inventories rebuild during the checkered recovery, and occupancy rates should begin to improve, assisted by extremely subdued development.

Weaknesses

Vacancy heads down from uncomfortably high midteen levels, but "we need a bunch of absorption to get to 8 to 10 percent." Despite reduced concessions, landlords will not gain pricing power again until late 2011 or into 2012 once occupancies increase above 90 percent. "We're dealing in a more drawn-out recovery with not enough demand to push rents." Rolling five-year leases coming off peak rents during the next two years will balance out any occupancy gains and tamp down net operating incomes, delaying a performance upturn. Investors must watch evolving changes in distribu-

EXHIBIT 4-9

U.S. Industrial/Distribution Investment Prospect Trends

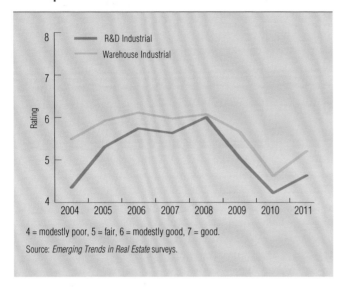

4 = modestly poor, 5 = fair, 6 = modestly good, 7 = good.

Source: *Emerging Trends in Real Estate* surveys.

EXHIBIT 4-10

U.S. Warehouse Industrial

2011	Prospects	Rating	Ranking
Investment Prospects	Fair	5.20	3rd
Development Prospects	Poor	3.13	3rd
Expected Capitalization Rate, December 2010		7.8%	

Buy	Hold	Sell
40.6%	52.6%	6.8%

Source: *Emerging Trends in Real Estate 2011* survey.
Note: Based on U.S. responses only.

EXHIBIT 4-11

U.S. R&D Industrial

2011	Prospects	Rating	Ranking
Investment Prospects	Fair	4.63	8th
Development Prospects	Poor	2.88	5th
Expected Capitalization Rate, December 2010		7.6%	

Buy	Hold	Sell
21.5%	61.6%	17.0%

Source: *Emerging Trends in Real Estate 2011* survey.
Note: Based on U.S. responses only.

EXHIBIT 4-12

U.S. Industrial Completions and Availability Rates

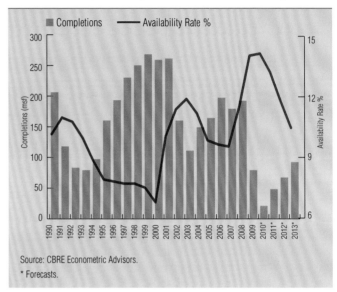

Source: CBRE Econometric Advisors.
* Forecasts.

tion models—not only the impacts of internet shopping and domestic point-to-point shipping, but also the consequences of a widened Panama Canal, increased railroad transport from expanding Mexican ports, and more presorted overseas exports.

Best Bets

Emerging Trends interviewees continue to tout familiar global trade seaport destinations: Los Angeles/Long Beach, San Francisco, Seattle, New York/New Jersey, and Miami. Houston and Dallas gain support from respondents who expect more shipping to be channeled through the Panama Canal and Mexico over the next decade. Canal widening will permit bigger ships from Asia to gain easier access to major Gulf and East Coast harbors. Houston stands to benefit, though its port is not deep enough to handle the largest ships, while Savannah and Norfolk prepare by deepening channels. West Coast ports could lose some market share, but given shipping trends, the United States desperately needs extra capacity to handle goods movement. "Don't be worried about L.A./Long Beach, where one third of import/exports are handled."

Avoid

Investors need to exercise greater care in placing their industrial bets. A "challenging and changing market" features "a ton of functional obsolescence," especially in shipping hubs where large tenants want taller and taller buildings "as racking tech-

EXHIBIT 4-13

U.S. Industrial Property Total Returns

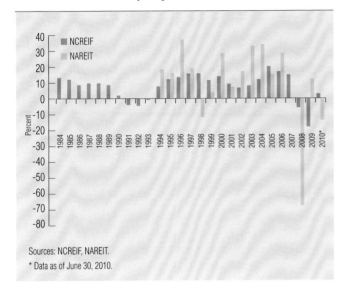

Sources: NCREIF, NAREIT.
* Data as of June 30, 2010.

nology gets better." Depending on oil prices, more long-haul, cross-country distribution could shift from trucks to railroads. "This could mean new distribution centers served by trains and shorter truck trips." The longstanding trend toward "fewer and bigger distribution centers may be in for a change."

Development

Hammered rents cannot "justify development, except for the odd build-to-suit." Until leasing rates spike 20 to 40 percent, depending on the market, new construction will continue to hover at or near record lows. Developers resign themselves to waiting until 2012 or 2013 before much activity resumes.

Outlook

Warehouse markets will bump along the bottom, firming slowly in a tepid recovery. Lukewarm consumer demand will not accelerate shipping and distribution, limiting the velocity of any leasing upsurge.

Research and Development

Traditionally volatile, specialized R&D markets typically make good buys close to the market nadir. When the economy inevitably gains strength, high tech, life sciences, and computer industries will be in the vanguard. That is why investors should scope out opportunities in brainpower bastions like Austin, San Jose, and Raleigh-Durham, as well as submarkets in Boston, Seattle's Silicon Forest, and the northern San Diego suburbs around La Jolla.

Hotels

Strengths

Hotels track back, thanks to modestly increased business and tourist travel rising off depressing nadirs. All key metrics—occupancies, room rates, and revenues—show improvement. "Hotels have the most flexibility to increase rates and can come back fastest." Operators "were geniuses at cutting costs" during the downturn—putting fewer towels in rooms, eliminating nighttime turndown service, shutting down elevators, you name it. "After the worst slump in decades, the outlook can only get better." Business-center hotels in gateway destinations enjoy the best prospects. "You can get some pop." The construction pipeline has mostly run dry, so new supply will not hamper recovery.

Weaknesses

Highly leveraged owners who bought late in the cycle get weeded out and many properties change hands. Deferred maintenance and capital expenditures leave facilities threadbare, tired looking, and needing upgrades. New owners must factor necessary and often costly improvements into budgets. Five-star properties struggle to attract enough profitable business to sustain substantial overheads; luxury lifestyles pare back, too. At the other end of the spectrum, extended-stay and roadside motels face oversupply. Better-capitalized owners can reduce rates and knock out competitors. Skittish lenders show little interest in providing financing to buyers. "There's no such thing as a safe loan on a hotel," says an insurance executive. "If you want to play, you might as well just own them. They are businesses, not property investments."

EXHIBIT 4-14

U.S. Hotel Investment Prospect Trends

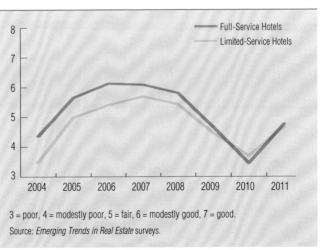

3 = poor, 4 = modestly poor, 5 = fair, 6 = modestly good, 7 = good.
Source: *Emerging Trends in Real Estate* surveys.

EXHIBIT 4-15
U.S. Hotels: Full Service

2011	Prospects	Rating	Ranking
Investment Prospects	Fair	4.77	6th
Development Prospects	Very poor	2.23	8th
Expected Capitalization Rate, December 2010		8.7%	

Buy	Hold	Sell
28.9%	52.4%	18.8%

Source: *Emerging Trends in Real Estate 2011* survey.
Note: Based on U.S. responses only.

EXHIBIT 4-16
U.S. Hotels: Limited Service

2011	Prospects	Rating	Ranking
Investment Prospects	Fair	4.67	7th
Development Prospects	Poor	2.58	6th
Expected Capitalization Rate, December 2010		9.0%	

Buy	Hold	Sell
26.6%	55.8%	17.7%

Source: *Emerging Trends in Real Estate 2011* survey.
Note: Based on U.S. responses only.

Best Bets

"Over the course of any decade, there are two years to buy hotels and two years to sell them. Now is the time to buy." But investors must fork over substantial equity and not get overly enamored of lobby decors or presidential-suite creature comforts. "This is a boom/bust property type," so prepare to sell quickly once any recovery takes hold.

Avoid

Buyers could overpay if they base pricing on a rapid return to peak occupancies and rates. "Those assumptions may not pan out," even in the top markets. Big-ticket resorts and high-end convention hotels will suffer as travelers and companies continue to count their pennies and downscale. Do not expect spendthrift flings and anything-goes travel budgets to come back in fashion anytime soon. Also, beware of gambling-related hotels and resorts. Too many Native American–operated casinos compete for dollars from exhausted consumers who do not have the luxury of losing any more money after recent housing and stock market declines. In particular, Las Vegas loses some glitz.

Development

Some lenders may consider financing an apartment project or a build-to-suit office for a high-credit corporation, but forget about a construction loan for a new hotel in the current environment: (virtually) no way.

EXHIBIT 4-17
U.S. Hotel Occupancy Rates and RevPAR

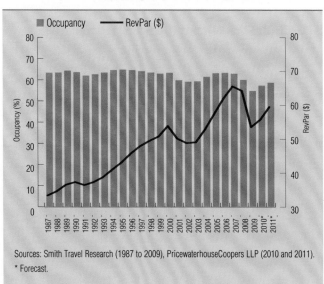

Sources: Smith Travel Research (1987 to 2009), PricewaterhouseCoopers LLP (2010 and 2011).
* Forecast.

EXHIBIT 4-18
U.S. Hotel/Lodging Property Total Returns

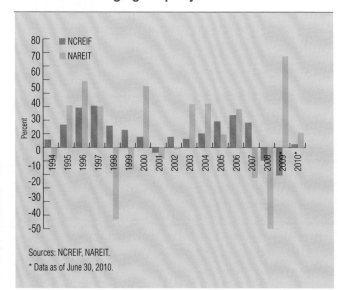

Sources: NCREIF, NAREIT.
* Data as of June 30, 2010.

Outlook

In an encouraging sign, "chocolates are back on pillows." But hotel performance correlates closely to growth in gross domestic product (GDP), and an expected elongated economic recovery bodes for a more-sluggish-than-typical resurgence in the lodging sector. Strong brands should attract more business: guests prefer to play it safe with tried-and-true innkeepers and make sure budgets go farther. Those reward programs help, too. "This sector is not for the faint of heart. You need a good operator."

Office

Strengths

"Not all office is created equal." Class A buildings in primary 24-hour markets remain highly coveted by tenants and investors. Corporate heavyweights and white-glove service firms still want the prestige and visibility provided by signature space. Cash-flush, high-net-worth investors and foreign buyers may gravitate to familiar skyline landmarks for ego benefits or out of familiarity, but these high-profile properties can hold values and sustain cash flows as well as any real estate subsector. Well-capitalized owners will continue to keep rollover tenants in place and lure existing tenants away from debt-ridden competitors, using improvement packages and free rent periods. "But some concessions begin to shrink—a good sign" for the overall market.

Weaknesses

Ugh. Where to begin? Outside of New York City, Washington, D.C., and a handful of other 24-hour downtown cores, few markets sustain a pulse, buried under high vacancies and falling revenues. "Demand is the worst I've ever seen." Companies turn ultra–cost conscious, expecting deals and wanting efficiencies, which "creates problems for landlords with older, more obsolescent space." Renewing firms rarely expand and either take the same amount of space or less, "not as a function of recession or one-time downsizing, but reflecting a new way of doing business and a focus on expense levels." More companies outsource and move jobs around on a global playing field to gain productivity advantages. "It's pervasive." Meanwhile, concessions eat into returns: "Face rents don't tell the story." Investors turn more wary, especially about commodity assets. "Office outperforms only at peaks; you need to time the market." They grow especially weary of inconsistent cash flows, high capital expenditures, inevitable concessions in market troughs, exposure to lumpy tenant rollovers, and "only narrow windows of profitability."

EXHIBIT 4-19
U.S. Office Investment Prospect Trends

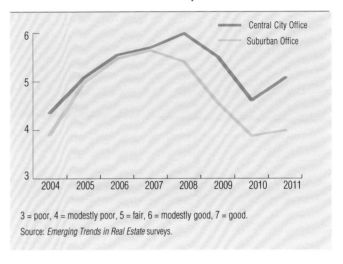

3 = poor, 4 = modestly poor, 5 = fair, 6 = modestly good, 7 = good.

Source: *Emerging Trends in Real Estate* surveys.

EXHIBIT 4-20
U.S. Central City Office

2011	Prospects	Rating	Ranking
Investment Prospects	Fair	5.08	4th
Development Prospects	Very poor	2.35	7th

| Expected Capitalization Rate, December 2010 | | 7.1% | |

Buy	Hold	Sell
34.7%	53.2%	12.1%

Source: *Emerging Trends in Real Estate 2011* survey.
Note: Based on U.S. responses only.

EXHIBIT 4-21
U.S. Suburban Office

2011	Prospects	Rating	Ranking
Investment Prospects	Modestly Poor	3.99	11th
Development Prospects	Very poor	1.83	11th

| Expected Capitalization Rate, December 2010 | | 8.3% | |

Buy	Hold	Sell
17.0%	53.1%	29.8%

Source: *Emerging Trends in Real Estate 2011* survey.
Note: Based on U.S. responses only.

EXHIBIT 4-22

U.S. Office New Supply and Net Absorption

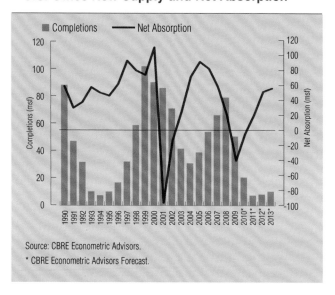

Source: CBRE Econometric Advisors.
* CBRE Econometric Advisors Forecast.

EXHIBIT 4-23

U.S. Office Vacancy Rates

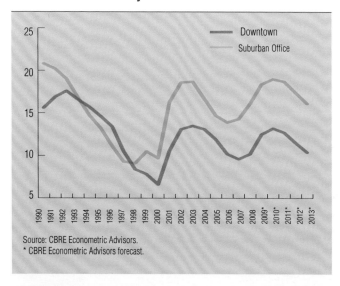

Source: CBRE Econometric Advisors.
* CBRE Econometric Advisors forecast.

Best Bets

Investors with sidelined cash will pursue the best properties in the best markets. "Even though it scares me that people use office less, it's hard to stay away from the best assets." Tenants should be "very motivated" to take advantage of low rents and concessions while they can. "We're several years away before landlords regain leverage over tenants, but at least it's moving more in that direction."

EXHIBIT 4-24

U.S. Office Property Total Returns

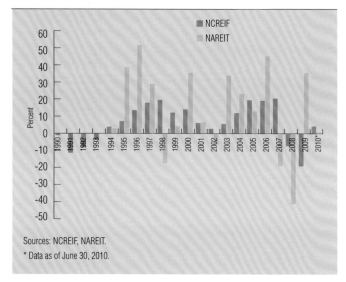

Sources: NCREIF, NAREIT.
* Data as of June 30, 2010.

Avoid

Suburban markets "could take years to recover" as occupancies slump in the low 80s "with no material demand drivers." Cutthroat leasing economics give away free rent and tenant improvements, slicing into net rents. "I can't imagine why anyone would want to own a suburban office building. It used to be back offices went to the suburbs. Now they go to India, Guatemala, Warsaw, or wherever." These "easy-to-build assets" turn into a "trading commodity." Owners have "no pricing power" over a cycle. The best you can hope for is "stabilized vacancies in the 10 to 15 percent range."

Development

On a market-enforced siesta, developers must carefully calibrate locating and timing their next buildings. History shows that following a downturn, early-out-of-the-ground projects have the best success. Usually they are completed into a wave of tenant demand. But this cycle may be different, if the nation's jobs engine does not ignite and companies stay in efficiency mode. Many secondary and tertiary markets will not attract enough growth to warrant much building activity. Developers instead focus more on infill locations near vibrant downtown cores and urbanizing suburban nodes, and realize new projects will need to go green.

Outlook

How much office space do we really need? Companies seem to "figure not as much." Expect only pockets of improvement, mostly in and around the global gateways. "Without employment growth, it's a zero-sum game. Somebody is winning at somebody else's expense." "Better buildings in better markets will fill up [vacancies] first," while B and C assets struggle and any "obsolescence deters leasing." Through 2011, tenants will look to trade up from Class B to A space and retain the upper hand in any lease negotiations. Inevitably, concession packages become less generous.

Retail

Strengths

Horrendously "low expectations haven't been met," and shopping-center investors regroup. "We're now realistically confident we can get through this rough period." Retailers closed weak stores and shed more than a million jobs, improving margins, enhancing inventory management, and making higher profits off smaller volumes. They now realign lineups in the best locations, benefiting fortress malls and prime infill community/power centers, but open smaller stores and command lower rents. At least "tenant seepage has stopped." Owners of good retail centers with high-credit tenants also can secure financing. "I'm surprised by how well it's held up." In a "survival of the fittest" environment, the strong not only endure, but fortify.

Weaknesses

Pessimism may have been overdone, but only by degrees. "Levels of concessions have been unprecedented. Malls look full, but owners forgive back rent, cap CAM [common-area maintenance] charges, or just let stores stay open without paying anything." Sales start to increase as shoppers concentrate buying activity in surviving locations, but overall, consumers do not spend enough. "We're limping along." Strong centers poach tenants from weaker malls. "It [the poaching] is open and notorious." For years, interviewees have wondered about America's "absurd" retail-space-per-capita ratios—the world's highest. Some gross leasable area will be wiped out across the shopping center landscape—anywhere from 5 to 10 percent. "If you drive around some suburban neighborhoods, everything is empty." Now malls and power centers lure supermarket chains into empty anchor locations—another blow to some already-shaky community centers, which have trouble meeting loan requirements or gaining access to refinancing capital. Internet

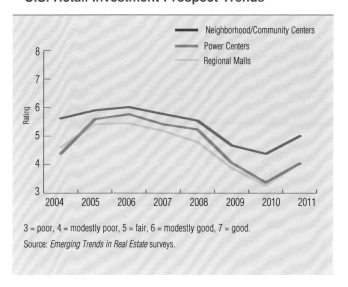

EXHIBIT 4-25

U.S. Retail Investment Prospect Trends

3 = poor, 4 = modestly poor, 5 = fair, 6 = modestly good, 7 = good.

Source: *Emerging Trends in Real Estate* surveys.

retailing already takes about a 10 percent market share away from bricks-and-mortar stores, with more to come. "People continue to spend less time in malls."

Best Bets

It is the same old story as during any flight to quality: investors want only the best properties—the best retailers, the best physical plant, and the best location. REITs long ago corralled most fortress malls and many prime grocery-anchored centers. Infill assets enjoy better prospects as retailers scout for more locations in urban and urbanizing districts. Secondary locations stay out of play "unless [the investments are] absolute steals," and there is only limited buyer interest in B/B+ malls. But savvy opportunistic investors may pick off some winners by recognizing the survivors. Any center with sales per square foot in the $250 range confronts change of use and redevelopment. Tenants, meanwhile, should use their ample leverage to lock in favorable deals.

Avoid

In the current climate, fringe retail strips, depending on mom-and-pop tenants, face longer odds. Regional malls under 1.5 million square feet lose ground as retailers concentrate in larger fortress centers. The lifestyle fad also seems to have run its course: a phenomenon of living large expectations diminishes in credit-starved times. Power centers with empty boxes may have trouble finding replacements.

EXHIBIT 4-26
U.S. Neighborhood/Community Centers

2011	Prospects	Rating	Ranking
Investment Prospects	Fair	5.05	5th
Development Prospects	Poor	3.05	4th
Expected Capitalization Rate, December 2010		7.6%	

Buy	Hold	Sell
41.5%	41.8%	16.7%

Source: *Emerging Trends in Real Estate 2011* survey.
Note: Based on U.S. responses only.

EXHIBIT 4-27
U.S. Regional Malls

2011	Prospects	Rating	Ranking
Investment Prospects	Modestly Poor	4.06	9th
Development Prospects	Very poor	1.84	10th
Expected Capitalization Rate, December 2010		7.2%	

Buy	Hold	Sell
12.6%	61.0%	26.3%

Source: *Emerging Trends in Real Estate 2011* survey.
Note: Based on U.S. responses only.

EXHIBIT 4-28
U.S. Power Centers

2011	Prospects	Rating	Ranking
Investment Prospects	Modestly Poor	4.04	10th
Development Prospects	Very poor	2.13	9th
Expected Capitalization Rate, December 2010		8.1%	

Buy	Hold	Sell
9.9%	58.8%	31.3%

Source: *Emerging Trends in Real Estate 2011* survey.
Note: Based on U.S. responses only.

EXHIBIT 4-29
U.S. Retail Completions and Vacancy Rates: Top 50 Markets

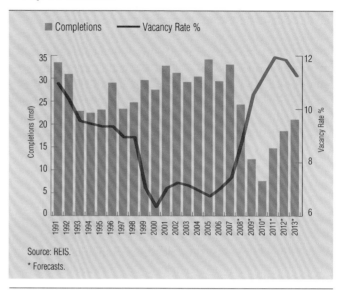

Source: REIS.
* Forecasts.

EXHIBIT 4-30
U.S. Retail Property Total Returns

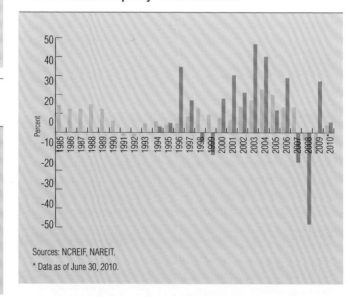

Sources: NCREIF, NAREIT.
* Data as of June 30, 2010.

Development

Simply nada. For the first time since the early 1950s, no regional malls are under construction in the United States. "That's stunning!" The big REITs focus on growth through consolidation, not building. Realistically, most areas need less retail, not more. "Endless strip construction is over." And some suburban shopping centers in densifying dis-

tricts must reinvent themselves. "We have the opportunity in this hiatus to rethink how we deliver retail in better transportation-linked urban centers, moving away from car-dependent models." Expect more mixed-use concepts involving residential space. "An aging population wants to drive less, and people in general want to shop closer to where they live." Any new development will focus on infill, rejecting big bets on emerging locations—but nothing happens in 2011.

Outlook

Shopping center owners could sustain a painful one-two punch. As a retrenching America buys less, more technologically enabled consumers also will reduce visits to traditional retail formats. Chain stores will morph into and be reconstituted with different concepts and looks, harnessing web innovations to drive more sales, whether online or in malls. Smaller stores in high-visibility, central locations—urban and suburban nodes—fit their parameters. Just like premier city shopping districts survived the post–World War II move to the suburbs, well-situated fortress malls and community retail will prosper in denser 21st-century suburbs. Probably more than any other property sector, retail braces for significant change.

Housing

Strengths

Housing markets may offer lessons for other real estate sectors: prepare for a long slog back to equilibrium after bouncing around on the bottom. Time and ongoing deleveraging will cure current imbalances, while forecast population growth will eventually sop up excess inventory so prices can advance (modestly). Low interest rates keep markets from getting worse and let high-credit borrowers reduce their mortgage costs. Not surprisingly, upscale neighborhoods in 24-hour cities and fashionable suburbs generally sustain values. Sound familiar?

Weaknesses

Misery engulfs many U.S. homeowners who overleveraged in a fantasy of ever-escalating values. The market crash erases not only "cash equity on which they were depending" to sustain lifestyles, but also (American) dreams of secure financial futures. "It takes a long time to recover lost value in a normalized market," let alone in an abnormally depressed one. Absent cheap credit, low early-year payments, and lackadaisical underwriting, many borrowers at all income strata could not really afford their homes and paid too much at inflated prices. "Perversely," people with bad credit who need help the most have been unable to take advantage of low interest rates to refinance or hold on to their homes as lenders belatedly tighten standards. Even worse, many potential homebuyers cannot muster enough equity to afford slashed prices and take advantage of the low mortgage rates. Some may be afraid to take the plunge given the unsettled jobs outlook, but many others have limited savings and debts to pay off—credit card, car loan, and mortgage. Trading-up buyers, a mainstay of transaction activity, cope with underwater mortgages on their existing homes, and lenders shut out speculators. "You can't get blood out of a stone."

Best Bets

For buyers with cash and sound credit, make no mistake: the time is right to acquire dream homes in dream locations. Market-bottom prices and record-low mortgage rates provide a unique opportunity to acquire assets at attractive discounts. You can have your pick of the right resort golf course hacienda or oceanside condo. Empty-nester parents can buy city digs for kids in preparation for downsizing out of suburban homes when markets look better. If you have money, you have plenty of options.

Avoid

Steer clear of tract mansions, "the Hummers of real estate." They never made much economic sense, given big heating bills, high property taxes, and large maintenance costs. "Now they're as obsolete as the cars." Housing in commodity subdivisions and more car-dependent areas may take decades to recover peak pricing.

Development

Good luck!

EXHIBIT 4-31

U.S. Single-Family Building Permits

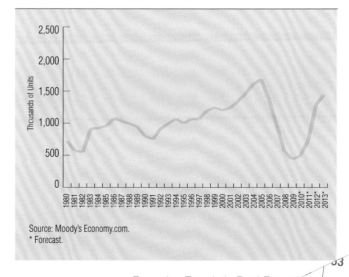

Source: Moody's Economy.com.
* Forecast.

EXHIBIT 4-32

The S&P/Case-Shiller Home Price Composite-20 Index

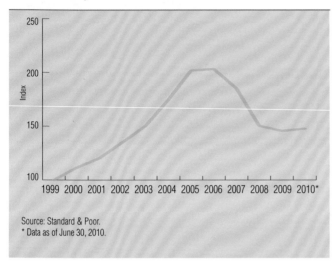

Source: Standard & Poor.
* Data as of June 30, 2010.

Outlook

Housing could stay in critical care well into 2012 or even 2013, until foreclosures and resale product clears. Only then can homebuilders resume activity, hoping that by then echo boomers with improved career prospects start to bail them out, buying at prices 30 to 40 percent off peaks. Shell-shocked by recent events, fewer people will be able to afford homes or feel comfortable owning them. Depending on what happens to Fannie Mae and Freddie Mac, mortgage spreads should widen and rising interest rates eventually will lead to higher borrowing costs. Underwriting standards will loosen, but purchasers will still need significant equity stakes and solid credit histories in the new world order. Developers have less success with greenfield subdivisions and concentrate on infill areas. Attached homes (townhouses) and other forms of in-town housing become more favored. Don't be surprised if more families rebond into intergenerational units—grandparents, parents, and grandchildren all living under one roof to share costs.

EXHIBIT 4-33

Prospects for Residential Property Types in 2011

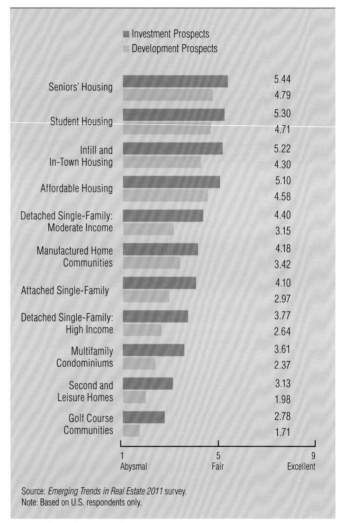

Source: Emerging Trends in Real Estate 2011 survey.
Note: Based on U.S. respondents only.

Niche Sectors

Retirement Housing

The common wisdom posits that bulging numbers of graying baby boomers will soon populate seniors' housing developments, which should be a major growth sector for builders. Indeed, seniors' housing registers relatively high scores for residential investment and development prospects in *Emerging Trends* surveys (see exhibit 4-33). But new realities may temper demand for retirement housing. "People wait longer to buy into seniors' facilities," says an interviewee. "Living longer and staying healthier, they enter retirement communities toward the end of life" when they have no choice "and don't stay as long." Now the economy pushes decisions further off. Compromised

Medical Office

As baby boomers age, physician visits will soar. Building and owning medical offices plays well into the expected demand wave. Investors concentrate activity around major hospital complexes. But this niche sector offers only a shallow pool of opportunities—more for local owners than institutional investors.

Student Housing

Echo boomers boast their own growing influence not only in multifamily, but also in student housing. Overflowing college campuses cannot handle demand in existing dorms, and older students prefer off-campus residences. Developers and investors should hurry: in about ten years, the number of college-age kids sharply declines.

Infrastructure

Considering compromised outlooks for commercial and residential sectors, many investors and developers contemplate possible growth schemes and take interest in infrastructure. More than 30 years of government underfunding and large deficits leave the United States in a major quandary for how to revamp and finance obsolete systems. Officials come to understand that a longstanding disconnect between local and regional planners, as well as a nonexistent national infrastructure strategy, leaves many metropolitan areas with inadequate roads, mass transit, and water resources to sustain future growth. Anticipate government leaders and institutional investors joining forces in trying to find solutions for the infrastructure dilemma through public/private partnerships. A national infrastructure bank, patterned on the post–World War II European model, and tax incentives for public/private partnerships could be among necessary initiatives.

EXHIBIT 4-34
Prospects for Niche and Multiuse Property Types in 2011

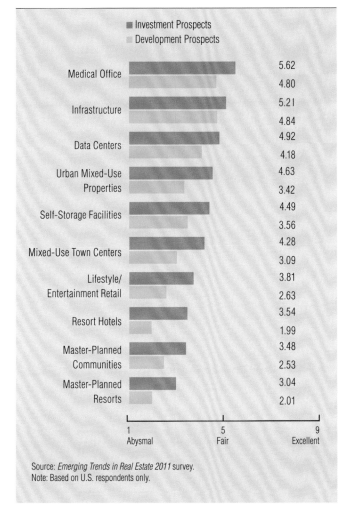

EXHIBIT 4-34

Prospects for Niche and Multiuse Property Types in 2011

Investment Prospects
Development Prospects

Property Type	Investment	Development
Medical Office	5.62	4.80
Infrastructure	5.21	4.84
Data Centers	4.92	4.18
Urban Mixed-Use Properties	4.63	3.42
Self-Storage Facilities	4.49	3.56
Mixed-Use Town Centers	4.28	3.09
Lifestyle/Entertainment Retail	3.81	2.63
Resort Hotels	3.54	1.99
Master-Planned Communities	3.48	2.53
Master-Planned Resorts	3.04	2.01

1 Abysmal   5 Fair   9 Excellent

Source: *Emerging Trends in Real Estate 2011* survey.
Note: Based on U.S. respondents only.

retirement savings and depleted pensions mean many seniors cannot afford seniors' housing and neither can their children, "so they stay in place or move in with kids for as long as they can." No doubt, more nursing home and elder care facilities will be needed over the next 20 years as leading-edge boomers hit the 85-year-old threshold. But in the meantime, living in pedestrian-friendly, 24-hour neighborhoods probably makes more sense than suburban residences for many ambulatory seniors: they maintain independence and can get to stores and doctors easily. Seniors' housing developers begin to reconsider strategies—pondering urban apartment residences and thinking twice about more typical landscaped suburban projects for younger seniors.

Emerging Trends in
Canada

"In Canada, real estate behaves as advertised, producing steady cash flow–oriented returns without much volatility, but an **ownership hold mentality** frustrates investors looking for opportunities to buy."

anada barely experienced recession and jolted into a V-shaped recovery. Now, 2011 promises slowing, steady growth and decent prospects for real estate investors as long as the U.S. economy does not drag them down. "Relieved" Canadian property owners and financial institutions cannot help contrasting their reasonably healthy condition with parlous U.S. markets. Fundamentals trend near equilibrium, "employment bounces back," and banks boast sound balance sheets. Most industries experience growth, including finance and energy, which helps support the service sector. "The domestic consumer has been pushing the economy, and jobs levels bounced back to prerecession levels. It's been phenomenal compared to the U.S."

Investment Prospects

U.S. Connection. Recent experience puts "Canada in a better place" and boosts confidence "that we can escape U.S. problems." Always linked to its more populous southern neighbor, the nation "tries to diversify" beyond a dependence on U.S. exports, extending trading relationships to Europe and Asia, particularly China. Still, a weak U.S. greenback and sputtering U.S. economy dampen cross-border commerce, hurting especially Ontario industrial markets, which serve Midwest manufacturing centers.

No Distress. The big difference for Canada has been the sound condition of its banks—"you can get a loan for anything"—since lenders maintained relatively strict underwriting standards and never were sucked into the CMBS maelstrom.

"We have no distress—no distressed banks, no distressed owners, no distressed sales." Now, rising interest rates coupled with tight bank requirements tamp down a recent home-buying spurt, particularly in Ontario and British Columbia, where purchasers stepped up activity before a new sales tax went into effect.

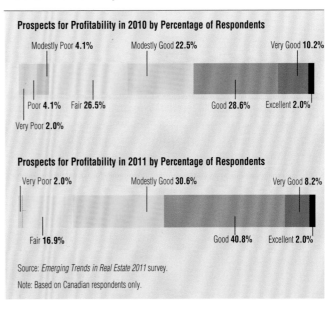

EXHIBIT 5-1
Firm Profitability Forecast

Prospects for Profitability in 2010 by Percentage of Respondents

Modestly Poor **4.1%**   Modestly Good **22.5%**   Very Good **10.2%**

Poor **4.1%**   Fair **26.5%**   Good **28.6%**   Excellent **2.0%**

Very Poor **2.0%**

Prospects for Profitability in 2011 by Percentage of Respondents

Very Poor **2.0%**   Modestly Good **30.6%**   Very Good **8.2%**

Fair **16.9%**   Good **40.8%**   Excellent **2.0%**

Source: *Emerging Trends in Real Estate 2011* survey.

Note: Based on Canadian respondents only.

EXHIBIT 5-2
Emerging Trends Barometer 2011

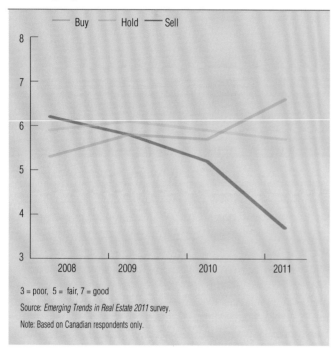

3 = poor, 5 = fair, 7 = good

Source: *Emerging Trends in Real Estate 2011* survey.

Note: Based on Canadian respondents only.

Investment Malaise. For 2011, "fundamentals should be okay, not great." Capital is back—"all the savvy players have dry powder"—and (as usual) investment opportunities will be limited; institutions dominate the major central city markets, holding on to assets for steady income instead of trading. *Emerging Trends* respondents exemplify the hold-on mentality: they think it is a good time to buy, but do not want to sell (see exhibit 5-2). "Bids are strong," says a broker, "but nothing's for sale." Investors "go crazy because there isn't anything to buy," and try to show discipline by walking away rather than overpaying for what is available. They have only slim chances to land discounted bargains—maybe off market in a fringe suburban district or a hotel where the owner has cash-flow problems. In this "compressing cap rate" environment, many deal-starved Canadians will be active in the United States, where they should have greater opportunity to spend their bankrolls and find higher yields.

EXHIBIT 5-3
Real Estate Business Prospects for 2011

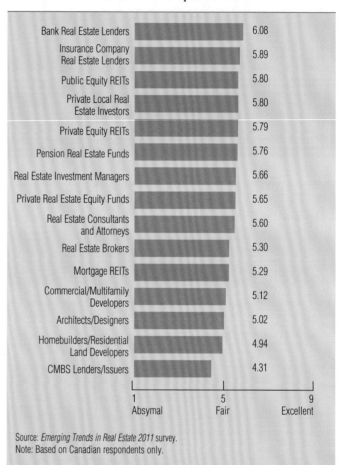

Source: *Emerging Trends in Real Estate 2011* survey.
Note: Based on Canadian respondents only.

Restrained Development. Except in Calgary, Canada's version of Wild West hot growth, builders have not overstepped. Imagine: "no large developers have gone bankrupt" in the country. North America's largest condominium market, Toronto keeps erecting high rises, but a greenbelt boundary to encourage denser neighborhoods helps support urban residential development. Toronto probably needs to take a breather in new office construction: four major new buildings come on stream. And the country does not need much additional retail space. Ontario typically provides good industrial development opportunities, but until the U.S. economy strengthens, sluggish demand does not support much new building. Pushed by municipal policies and code changes, Canadian developers increasingly buy into green building trends: "Anyone who doesn't embrace it will be economically imperiled."

EXHIBIT 5-4

Prospects for Capitalization Rates

Property Type	Cap Rate August 2010 (Percent)	Expected Cap Rate December 2011 (Percent)	Expected Cap Rate Shift (Basis Points)
Apartment Rental: High Income	5.92	5.74	-19
Apartment Rental: Moderate Income	6.24	6.06	-18
Central City Office	6.46	6.35	-10
Power Centers	7.01	6.66	-35
Neigh./Community Shopping Ctrs.	7.28	6.87	-41
Regional Malls	6.77	6.89	+13
Suburban Office	7.41	7.34	-7
Warehouse Industrial	7.58	7.56	-2
R&D Industrial	7.76	7.77	+1
Full-Service Hotels	8.67	8.68	+1
Limited-Service Hotels	9.15	8.98	-16

Source: *Emerging Trends in Real Estate 2011* survey.

Note: Based on Canadian respondents only.

Capital in Balance

Canadians admirably restrain any national gloating, but they can lay claim to having one of the world's healthiest capital markets. "Liquidity is back; no one's hard pressed." Except for some hotel owners, few borrowers confront refinancing issues. "In Canada, the real estate industry didn't get over-levered," and the markets never suffered any interruption of credit availability. Canadian banks benefit from a combination of institutional risk aversion and relatively stringent government regulation. Bankers prefer to credit their own discipline rather than regulator oversight: "We have fear of losing money." For whatever reasons, the system works, and the country and its consumers have "no credit hole to dig out of." During the past several years, "very cheap debt" propelled housing prices, but recent government interest rate hikes discourage further bubble formation, and lenders never sold exotic mortgage structures. Overall in 2011, *Emerging Trends* respondents expect a reasonable balance in debt market capital availability and an oversupply of equity capital, the result of nonsatiated buyers (see exhibit 5-5).

EXHIBIT 5-5

Real Estate Capital Market Balance Forecast for 2011

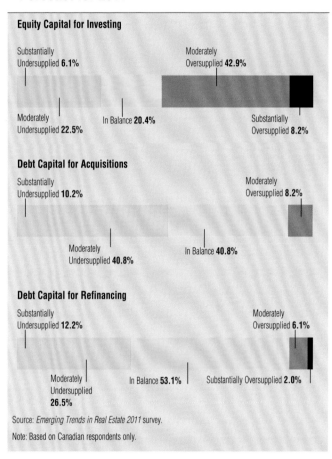

Equity Capital for Investing

Substantially Undersupplied 6.1%

Moderately Oversupplied 42.9%

Moderately Undersupplied 22.5%

In Balance 20.4%

Substantially Oversupplied 8.2%

Debt Capital for Acquisitions

Substantially Undersupplied 10.2%

Moderately Oversupplied 8.2%

Moderately Undersupplied 40.8%

In Balance 40.8%

Debt Capital for Refinancing

Substantially Undersupplied 12.2%

Moderately Oversupplied 6.1%

Moderately Undersupplied 26.5%

In Balance 53.1%

Substantially Oversupplied 2.0%

Source: *Emerging Trends in Real Estate 2011* survey.

Note: Based on Canadian respondents only.

Insurers and Pension Funds. A dominant handful of large insurance companies and public pension funds, which link liabilities to steady property cash flows, will continue to command ownership of the country's trophy commercial assets—downtown office space and regional malls. This story does not change.

REITs. Prices leveled off after strong run-ups in 2009. For 2011, analysts do not see "much room for big gains," and these stocks should stick close to valuations. Managements "can't significantly improve cash flow generation," but returns should be solid.

EXHIBIT 5-6
Equity Underwriting Standards Forecast for Canada

More Rigorous **35.4%**   Will Remain the Same **54.2%**

Less Rigorous **10.4%**

Source: *Emerging Trends in Real Estate 2011* survey.

Note: Based on Canadian respondents only.

EXHIBIT 5-7
Debt Underwriting Standards Forecast for Canada

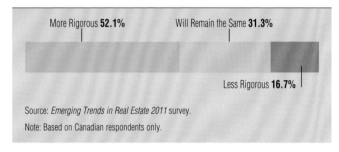

More Rigorous **52.1%**   Will Remain the Same **31.3%**

Less Rigorous **16.7%**

Source: *Emerging Trends in Real Estate 2011* survey.

Note: Based on Canadian respondents only.

EXHIBIT 5-8
Active Buyers/Acquirers of Real Estate in 2011

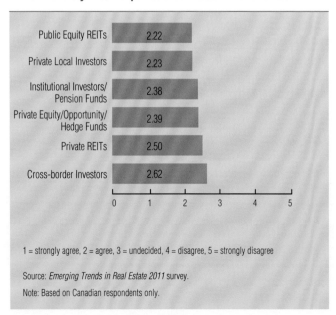

Public Equity REITs	2.22
Private Local Investors	2.23
Institutional Investors/ Pension Funds	2.38
Private Equity/Opportunity/ Hedge Funds	2.39
Private REITs	2.50
Cross-border Investors	2.62

1 = strongly agree, 2 = agree, 3 = undecided, 4 = disagree, 5 = strongly disagree

Source: *Emerging Trends in Real Estate 2011* survey.

Note: Based on Canadian respondents only.

EXHIBIT 5-9
Active Providers of Debt Capital in 2011

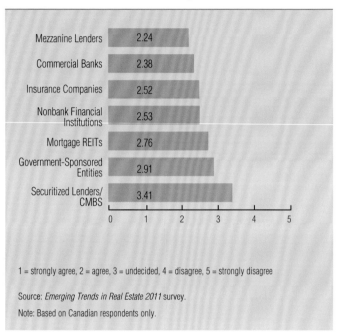

Mezzanine Lenders	2.24
Commercial Banks	2.38
Insurance Companies	2.52
Nonbank Financial Institutions	2.53
Mortgage REITs	2.76
Government-Sponsored Entities	2.91
Securitized Lenders/ CMBS	3.41

1 = strongly agree, 2 = agree, 3 = undecided, 4 = disagree, 5 = strongly disagree

Source: *Emerging Trends in Real Estate 2011* survey.

Note: Based on Canadian respondents only.

EXHIBIT 5-10
Preferred Strategy for Lenders

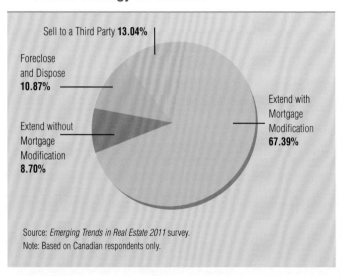

Sell to a Third Party **13.04%**

Foreclose and Dispose **10.87%**

Extend without Mortgage Modification **8.70%**

Extend with Mortgage Modification **67.39%**

Source: *Emerging Trends in Real Estate 2011* survey.

Note: Based on Canadian respondents only.

Foreign Investors. If it is not hard enough for domestic investors to find good acquisition opportunities, foreign players struggle even more to break in. "It's just hard to buy in Canada with markets dominated by a few players, so offshore investors can't build portfolios easily."

EXHIBIT 5-11
Canadian Markets to Watch

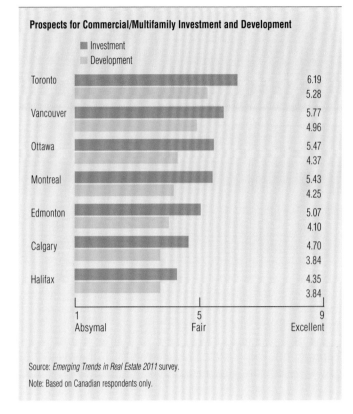

Prospects for Commercial/Multifamily Investment and Development

- Investment
- Development

	Investment	Development
Toronto	6.19	5.28
Vancouver	5.77	4.96
Ottawa	5.47	4.37
Montreal	5.43	4.25
Edmonton	5.07	4.10
Calgary	4.70	3.84
Halifax	4.35	3.84

1 Absymal   5 Fair   9 Excellent

Source: *Emerging Trends in Real Estate 2011* survey.
Note: Based on Canadian respondents only.

EXHIBIT 5-12
Canadian Markets to Watch Prospects for For-Sale Homebuilding

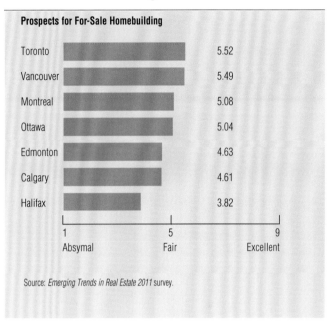

Prospects for For-Sale Homebuilding

Toronto	5.52
Vancouver	5.49
Montreal	5.08
Ottawa	5.04
Edmonton	4.63
Calgary	4.61
Halifax	3.82

1 Absymal   5 Fair   9 Excellent

Source: *Emerging Trends in Real Estate 2011* survey.

Markets to Watch

For 2011, major Canadian real estate markets settle in a fair to good investment range, with only modest investment prospects and constrained development potential. Toronto bumps Vancouver from the top ranking in the *Emerging Trends* survey, while Calgary must hope to recuperate from cooled demand and a touch of development binging. Population continues to concentrate in and around a handful of major 24-hour cores scattered from coast to coast, leaving extremely limited investment opportunities in small cities and rural areas in between. Shut out of primary cores, some investors scrounge for product in select secondary and suburban markets.

Toronto. Canada's "where-to-be market," Toronto stands out as a primary North American gateway and the country's most important economic engine. This vibrant metropolitan area radiates "lots of positives"—the rock-solid Bay Street financial sector and diverse manufacturing industries and service

businesses, as well as immigration flows to support growth. "We're hard to slow down." Some softness creeps into the office market as major tenants "play musical chairs" and move into new Class AAA development projects. No one gets too worried about vacated buildings because institutional owners will spend the necessary money to upgrade, reposition, and release space into future demand. Market vacancy will not increase materially above the current mid-single digits, and any near-term additional office development will be "small and niche." Observers wonder how the condo market just keeps expanding: new apartment projects pop up in all directions, fashioning one of the world's most expansive vertical skylines. Provincial policies encourage density in high-rise development south of a legislated greenbelt, which pressures demand. "We need approximately 40,000 new housing units to keep pace with population growth, but new projects provide less than 20,000." Smart money figured out "you can make a ton on infill land parcels," and anything near transit stations looks like gold. However, opportunities are few: "If you're already in the game and own, you can make a lot of money; if you're not, it may be impossible to get in." Some interviewees worry about flattening apartment rents as a surfeit of condo investors lease out units. High housing prices and immigration flows help make apartments a good bet. Investors retain interest in

EXHIBIT 5-13

Canadian Apartment Buy/Hold/Sell Recommendations by Metropolitan Area

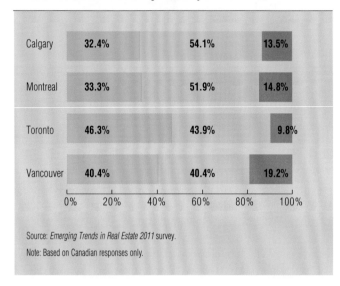

Calgary	32.4%	54.1%	13.5%
Montreal	33.3%	51.9%	14.8%
Toronto	46.3%	43.9%	9.8%
Vancouver	40.4%	40.4%	19.2%

Source: *Emerging Trends in Real Estate 2011* survey.
Note: Based on Canadian responses only.

EXHIBIT 5-14

Canadian Office Property Buy/Hold/Sell Recommendations by Metropolitan Area

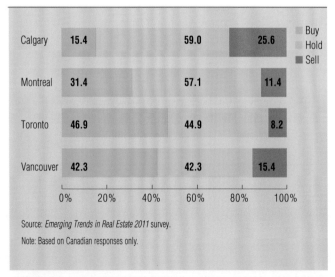

	Buy	Hold	Sell
Calgary	15.4	59.0	25.6
Montreal	31.4	57.1	11.4
Toronto	46.9	44.9	8.2
Vancouver	42.3	42.3	15.4

Source: *Emerging Trends in Real Estate 2011* survey.
Note: Based on Canadian responses only.

EXHIBIT 5-15

Canadian Retail Property Buy/Hold/Sell Recommendations by Metropolitan Area

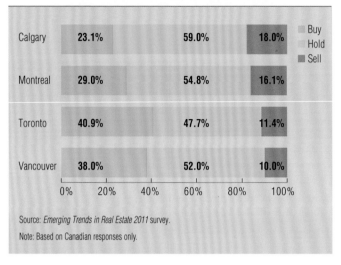

	Buy	Hold	Sell
Calgary	23.1%	59.0%	18.0%
Montreal	29.0%	54.8%	16.1%
Toronto	40.9%	47.7%	11.4%
Vancouver	38.0%	52.0%	10.0%

Source: *Emerging Trends in Real Estate 2011* survey.
Note: Based on Canadian responses only.

buying and holding industrial properties, which should recover from higher-than-average vacancies and rent declines once the United States gets untracked.

Vancouver. "Office and condo markets almost defy logic"; they stay "red hot." Instead of experiencing a post-Olympics dip, the city caught the attention of well-heeled international visitors, who stuck around and bought apartments after the games. "Everybody wants a view and waterfront location, but not everybody can afford it." Many wealthy Asians park money and look for a path to eventual citizenship. Institutional investors control the relatively small office market, which enjoys minuscule vacancies. Surrounded by water and mountain vistas, Vancouver's natural barriers control development and attract investors—a powerful combination. But some interviewees grow uneasy: "The market is artificially inflated; it's been too hot for too long." A new provincial sales tax raises costs and temporarily cools demand for midtier housing in some areas outside the core.

Ottawa. Canada's federal center offers low risk and little upside. "Nothing much changes." The government does not downsize, but the Canadian capital will never attract the same lobbying intensity or contractor-related business drawn to Washington, D.C.'s much more vast bureaucracy and

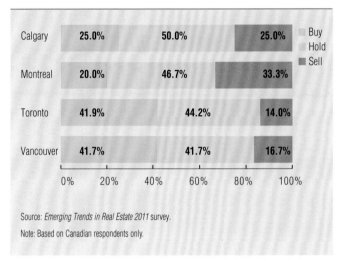

EXHIBIT 5-16

Canadian Industrial/Distribution Property Buy/Hold/Sell Recommendations by Metropolitan Area

Source: *Emerging Trends in Real Estate 2011* survey.

Note: Based on Canadian respondents only.

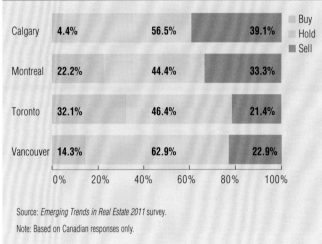

EXHIBIT 5-17

Canadian Hotel Property Buy/Hold/Sell Recommendations by Metropolitan Area

Source: *Emerging Trends in Real Estate 2011* survey.

Note: Based on Canadian responses only.

military/life sciences–related enterprises. A new convention center opens next year and could provide a potential market lift, especially for hotels and retail.

Montreal. Investors tend to short-shrift "slow and steady" Montreal in comparison with Toronto and Vancouver, but the market holds its own. "It's a good value" with "better yields." Besides mainstay Quebec provincial government offices, the city features a fairly diversified economy, including aerospace and financial services.

Edmonton. Edmonton "comes off a boil," avoiding the level of oversupply that deflates Calgary. Oil services businesses thrive because Canada strengthens its position as a leading supplier of oil and gas to U.S. markets. Locals expect positive impacts to filter through the economy, including employment growth.

Calgary. This market behaves more like a U.S. Sunbelt metro area than the typical Canadian 24-hour city. Sprawl and overbuilding "temporarily" subdue outlooks, but "absorption will come." Developers retreat in the face of high vacancies and show no appetite for new office projects. Locals put faith in robust commodities markets and U.S. consumption of oil from tar sands. "We may have a dirty process, but not comparable

to what happened with BP in the gulf." Expect spreading hot growth to resume in coming years; voters rejected a high-density-development greenbelt modeled after the one in Toronto.

Halifax. Off the radar screens of the big institutions, Halifax muddles along in slow growth mode. The Maritime Provinces fail to draw much new population and industry.

Property Types in Perspective

Reflecting modest expectations, property sector ratings improve over last year's tepid forecasts, especially for apartments and offices. Retail and industrial hold up, but hotels suffer from reduced U.S. tourist travel. Commercial markets promise to deliver cash flow but not much appreciation, while housing prices could ebb after an unsustainable surge. Most investors take heart in consistent metrics from markets, which linger in reasonable equilibrium; it beats writedowns, defaults, and foreclosures.

Apartments. Owners do not sell, and buyers bid up any multi-residence deal that comes to market—even older product. "You can't wrestle anything away from all the mom-and-pop landlords." Immigration fuels "high" tenant demand, while operators "fatten bottom lines" with cost controls, and overbuilding is a nonissue. Buying REIT stocks may be the best way to get a piece of this action. Some investors grow concerned about deferred maintenance on aging stock: "You need to factor capex into pricing."

Office. Occupancies trend well over 90 percent in all major markets except Calgary, where vacancies settle in the relatively manageable low teens. Even the best U.S. markets cannot come close to approaching these healthy supply/demand fundamentals. Rents generally stay in a narrow range without significant growth drivers. Pension fund owners "don't like vacancies," so they willingly make allowances in lease deals. In Canada, office investments behave the way core real estate is advertised, delivering reliable, income-oriented returns.

Retail. Shopping centers lease to capacity: "At 2 to 3 percent vacancies, they're essentially full." Low interest rates encouraged higher-than-normal levels of consumer debt, but most Canadians never caught credit fever and avoid going into hock. After only a mild recession, "we have decent consumer confidence and people feel good." Several U.S. department stores consider expanding across the border—"reinforcing already-strong demand for space"—but find few pad options at potential mall sites. Development activity focuses on small projects in infill areas; urban retail is undersupplied with stores, but land is difficult to find.

Industrial. Until U.S. exports increase, expect only "marginal improvement" in warehouse rents and occupancies, which begin to stabilize after a slump. "Owners work hard to fill empty space," but most are not overleveraged and can persevere through the turbulence. Seemingly insatiable investor demand appears unaffected by market softness. If owners get in trouble, they have ready exits. In Ontario, some warehouse markets outside of Greater Toronto face greater challenges, particularly Windsor.

Hotels. Lodging-sector fundamentals show signs of life, but need a bigger lift from American visitors, who stay closer to home. Some borrowers cry uncle and bail, giving cash investors a rare opportunity for bottom feeding.

Housing. Interviewees expect house prices to level off and soften, possibly slipping 5 to 10 percent, after a solid run. Rising interest rates and higher sales taxes in Ontario and British Columbia douse buyer fervor. The market had taken advantage of "free money"; now it's time to back off. Overseas purchasers buoy Toronto and Vancouver condo markets.

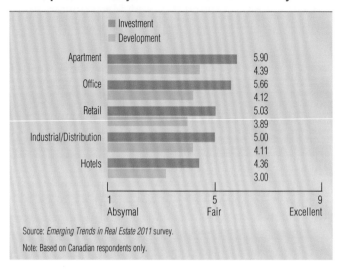

EXHIBIT 5-18
Prospects for Major Commercial/Multifamily

Source: *Emerging Trends in Real Estate 2011* survey.
Note: Based on Canadian respondents only.

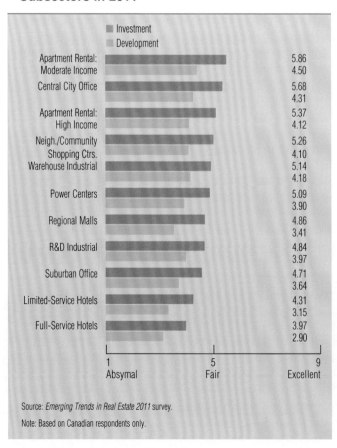

EXHIBIT 5-19
Prospects for Commercial/Multifamily Subsectors in 2011

Source: *Emerging Trends in Real Estate 2011* survey.
Note: Based on Canadian respondents only.

EXHIBIT 5-20

Prospects for Residential Property Types in 2011

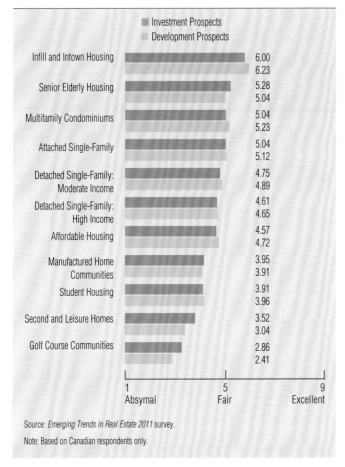

■ Investment Prospects
■ Development Prospects

Property Type		
Infill and Intown Housing	6.00	6.23
Senior Elderly Housing	5.28	5.04
Multifamily Condominiums	5.04	5.23
Attached Single-Family	5.04	5.12
Detached Single-Family: Moderate Income	4.75	4.89
Detached Single-Family: High Income	4.61	4.65
Affordable Housing	4.57	4.72
Manufactured Home Communities	3.95	3.91
Student Housing	3.91	3.96
Second and Leisure Homes	3.52	3.04
Golf Course Communities	2.86	2.41

1 Absymal   5 Fair   9 Excellent

Source: *Emerging Trends in Real Estate 2011* survey.

Note: Based on Canadian respondents only.

EXHIBIT 5-21

Prospects for Niche and Multiuse Property Types in 2011

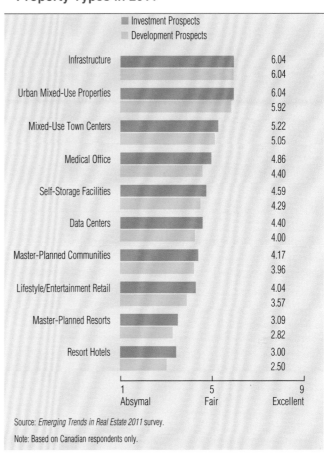

■ Investment Prospects
■ Development Prospects

Property Type		
Infrastructure	6.04	6.04
Urban Mixed-Use Properties	6.04	5.92
Mixed-Use Town Centers	5.22	5.05
Medical Office	4.86	4.40
Self-Storage Facilities	4.59	4.29
Data Centers	4.40	4.00
Master-Planned Communities	4.17	3.96
Lifestyle/Entertainment Retail	4.04	3.57
Master-Planned Resorts	3.09	2.82
Resort Hotels	3.00	2.50

1 Absymal   5 Fair   9 Excellent

Source: *Emerging Trends in Real Estate 2011* survey.

Note: Based on Canadian respondents only.

Best Bets

■ Winnow portfolios of select low-yielding assets and reinvest opportunistically in a U.S. market recovery.

■ Time investments to the market and buy down-but-not-out center city hotels.

■ Ditto on struggling industrial properties in the Greater Toronto area.

■ Buy apartments if you can find anything available. "They offer the best security."

■ Look for underperforming infill retail or commercial space, and position for redevelopment as condos. Canadian cities will continue to grow vertically as planners seek to encourage 24-hour environments.

■ Husband land sites inside the Toronto greenbelt for future residential development; demand and pricing should continue to increase.

EXHIBIT 5-22

Canada: Downtown Office Vacancy—Class A Space

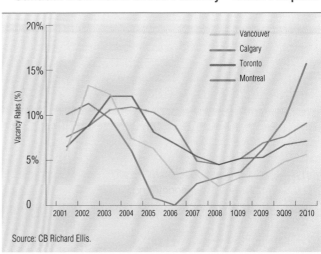

Source: CB Richard Ellis.

EXHIBIT 5-23
Canadian Central City Office

2011	Prospects	Rating	Ranking
Investment Prospects	Good	7.26	1st
Development Prospects	Modestly Poor	4.31	2nd
Expected Capitalization Rate, December 2011		6.4%	

Buy	Hold	Sell
41.9%	46.5%	11.6%

Source: *Emerging Trends in Real Estate 2011* survey.
Note: Based on Canadian respondents only.

EXHIBIT 5-24
Canadian Apartments—Moderate Income

2011	Prospects	Rating	Ranking
Investment Prospects	Modestly Good	5.86	2nd
Development Prospects	Fair	4.50	1st
Expected Capitalization Rate, December 2011		6.1%	

Buy	Hold	Sell
59.0%	35.9%	5.1%

Source: *Emerging Trends in Real Estate 2011* survey.
Note: Based on Canadian respondents only.

EXHIBIT 5-25
Canadian Apartments—High Income

2011	Prospects	Rating	Ranking
Investment Prospects	Fair	5.37	3rd
Development Prospects	Modestly Poor	4.12	4th
Expected Capitalization Rate, December 2011		5.7%	

Buy	Hold	Sell
38.5%	48.7%	12.8%

Source: *Emerging Trends in Real Estate 2011* survey.
Note: Based on Canadian respondents only.

EXHIBIT 5-26
Canadian Neighborhood/Community Centers

2011	Prospects	Rating	Ranking
Investment Prospects	Fair	5.26	4th
Development Prospects	Modestly Poor	4.10	5th
Expected Capitalization Rate, December 2011		6.9%	

Buy	Hold	Sell
34.2%	47.4%	18.4%

Source: *Emerging Trends in Real Estate 2011* survey.
Note: Based on Canadian respondents only.

EXHIBIT 5-27
Canadian Warehouse Industrial

2011	Prospects	Rating	Ranking
Investment Prospects	Fair	5.14	5th
Development Prospects	Modestly Poor	4.18	3rd
Expected Capitalization Rate, December 2011		7.6%	

Buy	Hold	Sell
31.7%	53.7%	14.6%

Source: *Emerging Trends in Real Estate 2011* survey.
Note: Based on Canadian respondents only.

EXHIBIT 5-28
Canadian Power Centers

2011	Prospects	Rating	Ranking
Investment Prospects	Fair	5.09	6th
Development Prospects	Modestly Poor	3.90	7th
Expected Capitalization Rate, December 2011		6.7%	

Buy	Hold	Sell
23.7%	63.2%	13.2%

Source: *Emerging Trends in Real Estate 2011* survey.
Note: Based on Canadian respondents only.

EXHIBIT 5-29
Canadian Regional Malls

2011	Prospects	Rating	Ranking
Investment Prospects	Fair	4.86	7th
Development Prospects	Poor	3.41	9th
Expected Capitalization Rate, December 2011		6.9%	

Buy	Hold	Sell
23.7%	73.7%	2.6%

Source: *Emerging Trends in Real Estate 2011* survey.
Note: Based on Canadia respondents only.

EXHIBIT 5-30
Canadian R&D Industrial

2011	Prospects	Rating	Ranking
Investment Prospects	Fair	4.84	8th
Development Prospects	Modestly Poor	3.97	6th
Expected Capitalization Rate, December 2011		7.8%	

Buy	Hold	Sell
21.1%	60.5%	18.4%

Source: *Emerging Trends in Real Estate 2011* survey.
Note: Based on Canadian respondents only.

EXHIBIT 5-31
Canadian Suburban Office

2011	Prospects	Rating	Ranking
Investment Prospects	Fair	4.71	9th
Development Prospects	Modestly Poor	3.64	8th
Expected Capitalization Rate, December 2011		7.3%	

Buy	Hold	Sell
18.4%	65.8%	15.8%

Source: *Emerging Trends in Real Estate 2011* survey.
Note: Based on Canadian respondents only.

EXHIBIT 5-32
Canadian Hotels—Limited Service

2011	Prospects	Rating	Ranking
Investment Prospects	Modestly Poor	4.31	10th
Development Prospects	Poor	3.15	10th
Expected Capitalization Rate, December 2011		9.0%	

Buy	Hold	Sell
12.1%	63.6%	24.2%

Source: *Emerging Trends in Real Estate 2011* survey.
Note: Based on Canadian respondents only.

EXHIBIT 5-33
Canadian Hotels—Full Service

2011	Prospects	Rating	Ranking
Investment Prospects	Modestly Poor	3.97	11th
Development Prospects	Poor	2.90	11th
Expected Capitalization Rate, December 2011		8.7%	

Buy	Hold	Sell
8.8%	64.7%	26.5%

Source: *Emerging Trends in Real Estate 2011* survey.
Note: Based on Canadian respondents only.

Emerging Trends in Latin America

Offshore investors see plenty of **potential** in two primary emerging markets, but various hurdles **limit** opportunities.

Where the United States has gone boom-bust and Canada offers only modest growth, Latin America's story centers on the enormous potential of two emerging markets—Brazil and Mexico. Together they account for two-thirds of the region's population "and most of its growth dynamics." But amid the swirl of young populations, an energized middle class, and the immense promise of expanding industries, investors deal with inevitable corruption and lack of transparency, the need to sort out the reliability of local partners, and—in the case of Mexico—the scourge of drug violence. Enticements and obstacles leave most North Americans intrigued by the possibilities, but not straying off home turf. In the United States, particularly, con-

tending with difficult domestic issues distracts from considering emerging market investments. But for those who do, the action is all about two countries: "They take the oxygen away from all other Latin American markets."

Brazil: Opportunities and Limits

Emerging Trends interviewees express few doubts: "The boom period has legs, the cat is out of the bag, people want to be where the action is, and that's Brazil." The country is self-sufficient in agriculture and energy, and expands its high-tech manufacturing. More offshore institutions "get their feet wet," but find limited opportunities in existing real estate because only a handful of buildings meet investment grade. Then they confront hurdles from Brazil's transaction culture of "group ownership," which makes deal making difficult. "It's hard to get all parties to sell."

Development may be where the real action lies. "There's a ton of demand for a ton of new space. You can build housing forever, and people will want it." Plus, shopping centers are few and far between, and distribution warehouse facilities are in short supply to serve growing consumer appetites. "The middle class is huge and dramatically increasing; populations concentrate in urban areas, creating intense demand for high-rise residential and retail." Again, local companies with big development platforms and insider connections have "a tremendous advantage and try to maintain a stranglehold; outsiders can't compete" and must make alliances. "Brave investors" enter secondary markets to develop malls, and strip centers will follow next.

EXHIBIT 6-1
Latin America General Indicators

	Unemployment (%)	Inflation (%)
Argentina	8.8	10.1
Brazil	6.8	5.1
Chile	9.1	2.0
Colombia	13.5	3.5
Ecuador	8.3	4.0
Mexico	5.2	4.6
Peru	8.8	1.5
Uruguay	7.4	6.2
Venezuela	6.6	29.7

Source: International Monetary Fund, *World Economic Outlook* database, April 2010; Moody's Economy.com.

EXHIBIT 6-2
Latin America Economic Growth

	Percentage Real GDP Growth						
	2007	2008	2009*	2010*	2011*	2012*	2013*
Chile	4.7	3.7	-1.5	4.7	**6.0**	4.8	4.6
Peru	8.9	9.8	0.9	6.3	**6.0**	5.7	5.7
Mexico	3.3	1.5	-6.5	4.2	**4.5**	5.2	4.9
Brazil	5.7	5.1	-0.2	5.5	**4.1**	4.1	4.1
Colombia	7.5	2.4	0.1	2.3	**4.0**	5.0	5.0
Uruguay	7.6	8.5	2.9	5.7	**3.9**	3.9	3.9
Argentina	8.7	6.8	0.9	3.5	**3.0**	3.0	3.0
Ecuador	2.5	7.2	0.4	2.5	**2.3**	2.0	2.0
Venezuela	8.4	4.8	-3.3	-2.6	**0.4**	0.5	1.6

Source: International Monetary Fund, *World Economic Outlook* database, April 2010.

* Projections.

EXHIBIT 6-3
Brazil: Foreign Direct Real Estate Investment

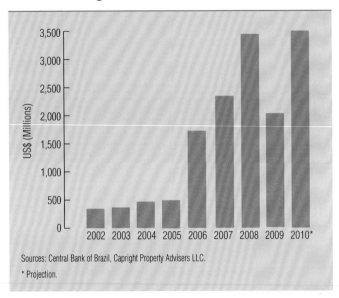

Sources: Central Bank of Brazil, Capright Property Advisers LLC.

* Projection.

For office markets, investors find an extremely limited menu in only two cities—Rio de Janeiro and Sao Paulo. "Everyone wants to be in Rio. The relatively small business district has virtually "zero percent vacancy," and rents skyrocketed "30 percent in the last year." The mountains-rising-from-ocean landscape leaves "no place to build," while the coming Olympics and World Cup fuel interest. Similarly, Sao Paulo's office sector remains tight, escalating rents and values. "It's a bubble driven by user demand, not speculators." Poor infrastructure limits new development opportunities. The city's roads and mass transit cannot handle population growth; 800 new cars each day add to already congested streets.

Interviewees expect yields to squeeze down, and markets to cool off but remain enticing. "Five years ago, investors expected IRRs [internal rates of return] of 40 percent. Now that's dropped into the high teens, and core funds are next."

Mexico: Potential and Concerns

Mexico offers obvious positives—a hard-working population, an expanding middle class, and the resulting increased demand for homes and consumer goods. But everybody reads about mind-blowing drug wars, police corruption, and political assassinations. In addition, real estate markets hit the skids when the U.S. economy tanked. Prices declined 30 to 35 percent and now recover—more than "halfway back"—but it's been "tough sledding."

Finally, banks relax lending curbs after "a huge liquidity crunch" brought on by the worldwide credit crisis. Mexican investors did not overborrow: patient equity players "take a patrimonial view" and count on long-term returns, relying on healthy demographics and controlled development. In fact, most cities and property sectors have avoided overbuilding. Boosters suggest that "markets now align" for significant growth from pent-up demand, and highlight opportunities to fill the remaining capital gap. "There's a large hole to fill," especially for construction loans. New laws allow domestic pension funds to invest in real estate and infrastructure, which could increase property market liquidity and demand for product. "We're seeing the checkbook at the end of the tunnel." But many jobs depend on the U.S. economy—manufacturing of time-sensitive products or heavy machinery that cannot be shipped by boat from Asia, hotel- and tourism-related businesses, and call centers. Locals necessarily raise concerns about when and whether the United States will emerge from its doldrums.

Industrial real estate "should improve during 2011" after a no-demand, no-development period. The U.S. downturn cuts two ways: overall declines in manufacturing and distribution activity, especially from "hardest-hit" northern border states, have been offset somewhat by more U.S. manufacturer relocations due to the weakened peso. Interior warehouse markets, serving Mexico City, suffered less. Retail "makes a good long-term play," betting on the growing middle class. Office markets show decent recovery and low vacancies in Mexico

City, but offer "negligible investment opportunities" because mostly domestic owners do not sell. Lenders require tenants in place for financing new construction, so "speculative development won't happen."

Most multifamily housing is owner occupied and heavily government subsidized. Developers receive a guaranteed return over ten-year periods without much upside. For-sale housing remains supply constrained by lack of construction financing, while the second-home market "went off the cliff" when U.S. retiree demand evaporated. Canadians fill some of the void, gaining buying power from their stronger dollar and the weaker peso. In favored coastal Baja and resort markets, cheap land could be a bargain. "The second-home market will come back."

Locals lament "too much distraction from drug issues," which torpedo revenues for some resort hotels already feeling the effects of U.S recession. "We need to deal with perceptions; it's our biggest hurdle to overcome." Other interviewees admit to "grim" security concerns, particularly in northern cities like Tijuana, Juárez, and Monterrey. "Business goes on, but not many relocations."

Government planners encourage future development to focus on more urban concepts and city centers, getting away from expanding suburban envelopes. The road-dependent sprawl model, copied from the United States, reaches the point of diminishing returns, creating hardships for many Mexicans who cannot afford cars or cannot support multicar households. Serious congestion and pollution, especially around Mexico City, must be addressed, too.

Interviewees

Abacus Capital Group LLC
Kyle Ellis
Benjamin L. Friedman

Ackman-Ziff Real Estate Group LLC
Gerald Cohen
Patrick Hanlon
Simon Ziff

AEW Capital Management
Marc Davidson

Allied Properties REIT
Michael Emory

The Alterra Group of Companies
Robert H. Cooper

AM Connell Associates LLC
Alice Connell

AMB Property Corporation
Guy Jaquier
Hamid R. Moghadam

APG Asset Management US Inc.
Steven Hason

Apollo Global Management
Joseph F. Azrack

ARA Finance
Thomas MacManus

The Arden Group
Craig A. Spencer

AREA Property Partners
Steve Wolf

Arnon Corporation
Gillie Vered

Artemis Advisors, LLC
Dale Anne Reiss

Aspac Developments Ltd.
Gary Wong

Associated Estates Realty Corporation
Lou Fatica

AvalonBay Communities, Inc.
Bryce Blair

Avison Young
Bill Argeropoulos
J. Richard Chilcott

Aviva Capital Management
Edward M. Casal

AXA Equitable
Timothy Welch

Ayer Capital
V. Raja

Babcock & Brown Residential
Philip Payne

Bank of America Merrill Lynch
Jeffrey D. Horowitz
Ron D. Sturzenegger

Barcelo Crestline
Bruce Wardinski

Barclays Capital
P. Sheridan Schechner
Ross Smotrich

Beacon Capital Partners, LLC
Sara Shank

Benchmark Assisted Living, LLC
Stephanie Handelson

Benenson Capital Partners
Richard Kessler

Bentall L.P.
Gary Whitelaw

Berkshire
David Olney
David Quade

Berkshire Property Advisors LLC
Larry Ellman

BlackHawk Real Estate LLC
Jamie Conoposk

Boston Properties
Mike Labelle
Mike Walsh

BPG Properties, Ltd.
Arthur P. Pasquarella

Brandywine Realty Trust
Gerard H. Sweeney

Brookfield Office Properties
Dennis Friedrich

Building Industry and Land Development Association
Stephen Dupuis

Buzz McCoy Associates, Inc.
Bowen H. "Buzz" McCoy

Calloway Real Estate Investment Trust
Simon Nyilassy

Camden Property Trust
Richard J. Campo

Campus Apartments
James A. Smith III

Camrost-Felcorp
David Feldman

Canadian Apartment Properties Real Estate Investment Trust
Thomas Schwartz

Capright Property Advisors LLC
Jay Marling
Selina McUmber

Carr Properties
Weston Andress

Carttera Private Equities Inc.
T. James Tadeson

CBRE Econometric Advisors
Jon Southard

CB Richard Ellis Ltd.
John O'Bryan
Raymond Wong
William C. Yowell III

Champion Partners
Jeff Swope

Citco–Real Estate Investment Fund (REIF) Services
Michael Peterson

City Ventures
Tony Pauker

The Clarett Group
Veronica W. Hackett

Claridge Homes
Bill Malhotra
Neil Malhotra

CNL Financial Group Inc.
Thomas K. Sittema

Colliers International
Ross Moore

Colony Capital, LLC
Richard B. Saltzman

Condor Properties Ltd.

Continental Development Corporation
Alex Rose

Cornerstone Real Estate Advisers LLC
Jim Clayton
David J. Reilly

Credit Suisse
Joshua Blaine
Boriana Karastoyanova

CRE Finance Council
Dorothy Cunningham

Crosland, LLC
Todd W. Mansfield

Crown Realty Partners
Michael Pittana

Cushman & Wakefield
James Carpenter
Bruce Ficke
Maria T. Sicola

Cushman & Wakefield Sonnenblick-Goldman
Steven Kohn

Developers Diversified Realty Corporation
David J. Oakes

DiamondRock Hospitality Company
Mark Brugger

Dorsay Development Corporation
Geoffrey Grayhurst

DRA Advisors, LLC
Gabe Levin
Paul McEvoy, Jr.

Dundee Real Estate Investment Trust and Dundee Realty Corporation
Michael Cooper

Dune Capital
Cornelia Buckley

Emigrant Bank
Patricia Goldstein

Empire Communities
Paul Golini, Jr.
Andrew Guizzetti
Daniel Guizzetti

Equibase Capital Group
Michael Husman

Equity Group Investments, LLC
Sam Zell

EVS Realty Advisors, Inc.
John Reis

Firm Capital Corporation
Eli Dadouch

First Capital Realty Inc.
Dori Segal

Forest City Commercial Group
James Ratner

Forum Partners
David Karp

GE Real Estate
Thomas Curtin
Michael Jordan
Ronald Pressman

GLL Partners
Dietmar Georg

Graywood Development Ltd.

Great Point Investors
Joseph Versaggi

GreenOak Real Estate Advisors
Sonny Kalsi

Greenpark Group of Companies
Carlo Baldassarra

Grosvenor Investment Management US, Inc.
Douglas S. Callantine

Grubb & Ellis
Robert Bach

Guggenheim Real Estate
Joe Mahoney

H/2 Capital Partners
Spencer Haber

Harbor Group International
Richard Litton
Lane Shea

Hawkeye Partners L.P.
Bret R. Wilkerson

Heitman
Richard Kateley

High Street Equity Advisors
Bob Chargares

HIGroup, LLC
Douglas Cameron

Hilton Worldwide
Christopher J. Nassetta

Hines
Ken Hubbard

HOOPP
Michael Catford

Hopewell Development Corporation
Lesley Conway
Kevin Pshebniski

Houlihan Lokey
Jonathan G. Geanakos

Humphreys Real Estate Investments
Kirk Humphreys

Hyde Street Holdings, LLC
Patricia R. Healy

ING Clarion Partners
Chuck Lathem

Institutional Real Estate, Inc.
Geoffrey Dohrmann

International Council of Shopping Centers
Mike Kercheval

I-Star Financial
George Puskar

John Buck Company
Charlie Beaver
Steven Shiltz
Kent A. Swanson

JP Morgan Asset Management
Jean M. Anderson
Mark Bonapace
Sheryl M. Crosland
Kevin Faxon
Mike P. Kelly
Michael O'Brien
Anne S. Pfeiffer
Elizabeth T. Propp
Frederick N. Sheppard
James M. Walsh

Kennedy Associates Real Estate Counsel
Douglas Poutasse
Preston Sargent

Kimco Realty Corporation
Michael V. Pappagallo

KingSett Capital Inc.
Jon Love

Korpacz Realty Advisors
Peter Korpacz

KTR Capital Partners
Robert Savage

Lachman Associates
Leanne Lachman

LaSalle Investment Management
Lynn Thurber

LEM Mezzanine LLP
Herb Miller

Liberty Property Trust
Michael T. Hagan

Lubert-Adler Partners
David Solis Cohen

Macquarie Capital Inc.
Simon Breedon

Macquarie Capital Funds, Inc.
Mark Mullen

Madison Homes
Miguel Singer

Madison International Realty
Ronald M. Dickerman

Manulife Financial
Constantino "Tino" Argimon
David Shaw
Joseph D. Shaw
Ted Willcocks

Mattamy Homes
Peter E. Gilgan

Melcor Developments Ltd.
Ralph B. Young

Menkes Developments Ltd.
Peter Menkes

Mesirow Financial
Chris Helmetag
Greg Karczewski

Metrus Properties
Robert DeGasperis

Metzler Realty Advisors, Inc.
Donald Wise

Midway Companies
Brad Freels

Monday Properties
Anthony Westreich

Moody's Investors Service
Merrie Frankel

Moran and Company
Mary Ann King

Morgan Properties
Mitchell L. Morgan

Mount Kellett Capital Management L.P.
Kevin Naughton

National Association of Real Estate Investment Managers
Stephen M. Renna

National Association of Real Estate Investment Trusts
Steven A. Wechsler

New Boston Fund, Inc.
Mike Doherty
Tim Medlock
Jim Rappaport
Kirk Sykes
David Willett

New Tower Trust
Patrick O. Mayberry

Northwestern Mutual Life Insurance Co.
David D. Clark

O'Connor Capital Partners
Thomas Quinn
Joseph M. Zuber

Otéra Capital
Ross Brennan

Oxford Properties Group
Blake Hutcheson

Pennsylvania Real Estate Investment Trust
Daniel G. Donley
Jeffrey A. Linn
Joshua G. Schrier

PM Realty Group
John S. Dailey

PNC Real Estate Finance
William G. Lashbrook

Portfolio Advisors
Harry Pierandri

Praedium Group LLC
Russell L. Appel

Principal Real Estate Investors
Michael J. Lara
Andrew Warren

Prudential Real Estate Investors
J. Allen Smith

PSP Investments
Neil Cunningham

Pyramid Advisors
Chris Devine
Rick Kelleher
Jack Levy

Quadrant Real Estate Advisors
Thomas Mattinson

RBC Capital Markets
Carolyn Blair
Daniel Giaquinto
Douglas McGregor

The Real Estate Roundtable
Jeffrey DeBoer

RealNet Canada
George Carras

Real Property Association of Canada
Michael Brooks

Regency Centers Corporation
Martin E. Stein, Jr.

Regent Partners
David Allman

RioCan Real Estate Investment Trust
Edward Sonshine
Frederic Waks

Rockwood Capital
Arne Arnesen

Rockwood Mexico
Blanca Rodriguez

Rosen Consulting Group
Kenneth Rosen

Rothschild Realty
D. Pike Aloian

RREEF
Scott Koenig
Charles B. Leitner
Kurt W. Roeloffs

RXR Realty LLC
Frank Patafio

Savills, LLC
Allison Bradshaw
Jeffrey Cooper
John D. Lyons
Gerard Mason
Arthur Milston
R. John Wilcox

Sentinel Real Estate Corporation
David Weiner

Seven Hills Properties
Luis A. Belmonte

Shenkman Corporation
Kevin E. McCrann

SL Green Realty Corporation
Isaac Zion

Softec
Gene Towle

Sonnenblick-Eichner Company
David Sonnenblick

The Sorbara Group
Edward Sorbara
Joseph Sorbara

Square Mile Capital Management LLC
Jeffrey Citrin
Craig Solomon

Stag Capital Partners
Ben Butcher

Starwood Capital Group
Jeffrey Dishner
Jerry Silvey

Taggart Realty Management
Jeff Parkes
Michelle Taggart
Paul Taggart

Thompson National Properties LLC
Anthony Thompson

Timbercreek Asset Management
Ugo Bizzari

Trademark Property Company
Terry R. Montesi

TRECAP Partners
Robert Fabiszewski
Michael McNamara
Douglas Tibbetts

Tricon Capital Group Inc.
David Berman
Gary Berman

TriLyn LLC
Mark Antoncic

TriMont Real Estate Advisors
Brian Pittard
Greg Winchester

Trinity Capital Advisors
Sean J. McKinley

Trinity Real Estate
Richard Leider

UBS Global Asset Management (Americas) Inc.
Lee S. Saltzman

UBS Realty Investors LLC
Matthew Lynch

University of Denver, Dividend Capital Group
Glenn Mueller

Urban America
Tom Kennedy

USAA Real Estate Company
T. Patrick Duncan

U-Store-It Trust
Christopher P. Marr

Valtus Capital Group
John Gilchrist
Michael Jabara
Viney Singal

Vantage Real Estate Partners
Ryan Gilbert

Verde Realty
Jeannette Rice

Virginia Retirement System
Field Griffith

Vornado Realty Trust
Michael D. Fascitelli

Walker & Dunlop
Kieran Quinn

Washington Real Estate Investment Trust
Thomas Regnell

Weingarten Realty
Gary Greenberg

Wells Fargo
Charles H. "Chip" Fedalen, Jr.

Wells Real Estate Funds
Don Henry

Welsh Capital, LLC
Peter C. Austin

Westbank Projects Corp.
Judy Leung

Westbrook Partners
Sush Torgalkar

Westfield Capital Partners
Ray D'Ardenne

Wright Runstad & Company
Gregory K. Johnson

Sponsoring Organizations

PricewaterhouseCoopers real estate practice assists real estate investment advisers, real estate investment trusts, public and private real estate investors, corporations, and real estate management funds in developing real estate strategies; evaluating acquisitions and dispositions; and appraising and valuing real estate. Its global network of dedicated real estate professionals enables it to assemble for its clients the most qualified and appropriate team of specialists in the areas of capital markets, systems analysis and implementation, research, accounting, and tax.

Global Real Estate Leadership Team

Barry Benjamin
Global Asset Management Leader
Luxembourg, Luxembourg

Kees Hage
Global Real Estate Leader
Luxembourg, Luxembourg

Uwe Stoschek
Global Real Estate Tax Leader
Berlin, Germany

Timothy Conlon
United States Real Estate Leader
New York, New York, U.S.A.

Paul Ryan
United States Real Estate Tax Leader
New York, New York, U.S.A.

Mitchell M. Roschelle
United States Real Estate Business Advisory Services Leader
New York, New York, U.S.A.

K.K. So
Asia Pacific Real Estate Tax Leader
Hong Kong, China

John Forbes
European, Middle East & Africa Real Estate Leader
London, England, United Kingdom

www.pwc.com

Urban Land Institute

The mission of the Urban Land Institute is to provide leadership in the responsible use of land and in creating and sustaining thriving communities worldwide. ULI is committed to
■ Bringing together leaders from across the fields of real estate and land use policy to exchange best practices and serve community needs;
■ Fostering collaboration within and beyond ULI's membership through mentoring, dialogue, and problem solving;
■ Exploring issues of urbanization, conservation, regeneration, land use, capital formation, and sustainable development;
■ Advancing land use policies and design practices that respect the uniqueness of both built and natural environments;
■ Sharing knowledge through education, applied research, publishing, and electronic media; and
■ Sustaining a diverse global network of local practice and advisory efforts that address current and future challenges.

Established in 1936, the Institute today has nearly 30,000 members worldwide, representing the entire spectrum of the land use and development disciplines. ULI relies heavily on the experience of its members. It is through member involvement and information resources that ULI has been able to set standards of excellence in development practice. The Institute has long been recognized as one of the world's most respected and widely quoted sources of objective information on urban planning, growth, and development.

Patrick L. Phillips
Chief Executive Officer, Urban Land Institute

Urban Land Institute
1025 Thomas Jefferson Street, NW
Suite 500 West
Washington, DC 20007
202-624-7000
www.uli.org